I0004781

Reg's Practical Guide To Understanding Windows 7

By Reginald T. Prior

Copyright © 2009 by Reginald T. Prior

Cover design by Reginald T. Prior
Book design by Reginald T. Prior

All rights reserved.

No part of this book may be reproduced in any form or by any electronic or mechanical means including information storage and retrieval systems, without permission in writing from the author. The only exception is by a reviewer, who may quote short excerpts in a review.

Reginald T. Prior

Visit http://www.rcsbooks.com or E-Mail me at reginaldprior@gmail.com

Printed in the United States of America

First Printing: October 2009

ISBN - 1453861319
EAN - 139781453861318

Trademarks And Copyrights

Trademarked and or copyrighted names appear throughout this book. Rather than list and name the entities, names or companies that own the trademark and or copyright or insert a trademark or copyright symbol for with every mention of the trademarked and or copyrighted name, The publisher and the author states that it is using the names for editorial purposes only and to benefit the trademark and or copyright owner, with no intentions of infringing on the trademark and or copyrights.

Warning and Disclaimer

Every effort has been made to make this book as complete and accurate as possible. No warranties are implied. The information provided is on a "as is" basis. The author and the publisher has no liability or responsibility to any individuals or entities with any respect to any loss or damages from the information provided in this book or from the use of the utilities CD or any programs on it.

Preface

There are many books on the market that teach people how to use their computers. But as I look through these books, I found that they teach some of the tasks about operating their computers, but miss a lot of critical things about fully utilizing their computers. Also I found with a lot of these books that they do not fully explain computer terminology at all in laymen's terms or teach people how to backup and restore their critical data (Documents, Pictures, etc) on their computers in case of a computer malfunction or viruses attacking their computer.

My aim of this book is to fill in these gaps in computer literacy that most books do not cover or spend sufficient time covering in common sense and in a way that is easily understood by everyone. As a computer technician for 12 years, I have come across many people that understand some things about computers, but want to have a better understanding about how they work and to fully utilize them in their everyday lives.

In this book, I will be covering the Microsoft Windows 7 Operating System. At the time of the writing this book, this is the latest operating system that was released from Microsoft to the world. There are major differences in Windows 7 than in XP or Vista. But some things from the previous versions of Windows remain the same. The changes and the things that remain the same are explained so that you can easily follow along the with the lessons in this book.

You as the reader are the most important critics of this book. I value all of your feedback and suggestions that you may have for future books and other things that I can do to make these books better. You can e-mail me at reginaldprior@gmail.com and please include the book title, as well as your name and e-mail address. I will review your comments and suggestions and will keep these things in mind when I write future texts. Thank you in advance,

Reginald T. Prior

Acknowledgements

This book that you are reading right now takes a lot of time and sacrifice to put together. I would first and foremost thank God for giving me at the age of six the love of working on computers that still is as strong today as it was back then. I would like to thank my wife, Sharifa for being a trooper when I was spending many hours on my laptop putting this book together and also for being there to help me read my drafts to make sure that it would be understood.

Also I would like to thank my family and many friends that helped and supported me throughout the years on many other projects and being there for me in good times and bad. I hope that you all enjoy this book as much as I had putting it together.

Hello Everyone,

I would like to thank you in advance for purchasing "Reg's Practical Guide To Understanding Windows 7" Like my last book "Reg's Practical Guide To Understanding Computers" that mainly focused on Microsoft's Windows XP and Vista operating systems, I aim to make the newly released Windows 7 operating system easy to learn while showing you the newest features and other changes that Microsoft has made to make this version of Windows the best yet.

If you just look at screenshots of Windows 7 and Windows Vista side by side, you would think that they are the same operating system and Microsoft is just re-releasing Vista, but under a different name. I want to let you know that after testing the beta version of Windows 7, Microsoft has made wholesale and drastic changes to Windows 7 that make this version of Windows as advertised "The best Windows yet" I will go over just about all of the changes in this book, because it is a lot of them.

The small list of overall changes includes:

1. Jump Lists which better organize your taskbar (Sort of like stacks in the Apple Macintosh operating system)

2. Taskbar previews that actually work (Was supposed to work with Vista)

3. Home Group which simplifies sharing your printer or files with other computers in your home through a wireless network

4. Overall faster and simpler to use than Windows Vista

5. Reverse Compatibility with Windows XP software and drivers for hardware with the new XP-Mode (Only in the Professional And Ultimate Versions Of Windows 7) where if a program you have does not initially work with Windows 7, you can run a virtual copy of XP in the background to make it work.

And this is just some of the changes with Windows 7. I will explain in more detail later in this book.

Before you buy and install Windows 7 for your current computer or plan on purchasing a new computer to use Windows 7, your computer(s) need to have the following specs to be able to fully take advantage of this great operating system:

1. At least a 80 Gigabytes of hard drive space
2. 2 to 4 Gigabytes of Ram (Memory)
3. 128MB or more of Video Ram (Memory)
4. 1.5Ghz or Faster Processor

I know what you must be saying to yourself as you read that last section, "here we go with that techie speak" Like I stated on the last page, My aim of this book is to help you understand computers and that also includes meanings of the techie speak. Chapter One is dedicated to making you understand the computer tech language so that you will be able to understand what to look for.

Well, without anymore delays, lets get into why you purchased this book, and that is to learn about and take advantage of Windows 7!

Comparisons between All Windows 7 Versions

	Home Premium	Professional	Ultimate
What does it take to run Windows 7?			
Features			
See more features			
Make the things you do every day easier with improved desktop navigation.	✓	✓	✓
Start programs faster and more easily, and quickly find the documents you use most often.	✓	✓	✓
Make your web experience faster, easier and safer than ever with Internet Explorer 8.	✓	✓	✓
Watch, pause, rewind, and record TV on your PC.	✓	✓	✓
Easily create a home network and connect your PCs to a printer with HomeGroup.	✓	✓	✓
Run many Windows XP productivity programs in Windows XP Mode.		✓	✓
Connect to company networks easily and more securely with Domain Join.		✓	✓
In addition to full-system Backup and Restore found in all editions, you can back up to a home or business network.		✓	✓
Help protect data on your PC and portable storage devices against loss or theft with BitLocker.			✓
Work in the language of your choice and switch between any of 35 languages.			✓

Table Of Contents:

Chapter One: Computer Terminology Dictionary

Computer Terminology Dictionary --10
How To Turn Your Computer On And Off -- 15

Chapter Two: Getting Acquainted With the Windows® 7 Desktop And Changes

Getting Around The Desktop And Changes For Windows 7------------------------------ 18
Changing Desktop Background -- 22
Creating Custom Themes --23
Sharing Custom Themes With Friends And Family --28
Changing/Configuring Your Screensaver -- 29
Searching For Things On Your Computer -- 31
The Shortcuts/Open Programs Area Of The Windows Toolbar ---------------------------- 32
Using The New Windows 7 Jump Lists Feature ---33
The Notification Area Of The Windows Toolbar -- 34
Changing Time/Date On Your Computer --36
Using The Recycle Bin -- 37
Adding/Changing Users In Windows -- 38
Reading Windows Pathnames -- 41

Chapter Three: Basic Internet Browsing

Internet Lingo, Web Terminology --47
Getting Connected To Wireless Internet Connections --48
Parts Of Your Web Browser --49
Using Search Providers/Engines To Find Things On The Internet -------------------------------50
Using Bookmarks/Favorites ---52
Changing Default Web Page When Your Browser Loads --53

Chapter Four: Using and Fully Utilizing Electronic Mail (E-Mail)

Setting Up Your E-Mail Account On Outlook Express --57
The Main Screens Of Your E-Mail Program ---59
Sending E-Mails --60
Sending Attachments In E-Mails --61
Opening And Replying To E-Mails --62
Forwarding, Deleting E-Mails --------------------------------- ------------------------------63
Using Your Contact/Address Book --63
Adding Signatures To Your E-Mails --65

Chapter Five: The Critical Task of Backing up Your Computer

Using Fab's Autobackup To Simplify Backing Up Your Computer -------------------------------68
Restoring Your Backups With Fab's Autobackup --74

Chapter Six: Computer Maintenance and Upkeep

Importance Of Having Current Antivirus Programs Updated --78
Importance Of Having Current Anti-Spyware Programs Updated --79
Dangers Of Using Peer To Peer Software Like Limewire, etc ---82

Chapter Seven: Taking Back Control Of Your Computer

Why You Should Take Charge Of Your Computer ------------------------- --------------------------------- ----86
First Phase – Time Restrictions --------------------------------------- -------------------------------------87
Second Phase – Limiting Access To Computer Programs ----- --90
Third Phase – Filtering Internet Websites --92

8

Chapter One:

Computer Terminology Dictionary

Chapter One: Computer Terminology Dictionary

Before we go into learning how to operate Windows or Computers in general, I believe that before you can build knowledge in anything, we have to build your knowledge like a builder builds a house. First we have to have a solid foundation laid down before we can start building floors and rooms within the house. Fully understanding computer terminology and knowing what it means is like laying the foundation on the house.

Many people get confused when they hear specific questions about their computer to help solve issues such as "How much RAM do you have on your computer" or "How much hard drive space does your computer have" either the person has no idea what we are talking about and say that this is a foreign language or the person tells the tech the hard drive space specs instead of the RAM or vice versa.

This chapter translates what us geeks talk about when we are talking about a computer. Decode the foreign language so to speak. This is not a full list of computer terminology, which would be a book by itself. But this is a list of the most common terminology used for talking about computers. So with no further delays, lets get started laying the foundation to being confident to speak "Computer Language".

Computer Terminology

Hardware

Hardware is the actual pieces of the computer that you can see and touch. A computer monitor is considered hardware, a computer tower or laptop are hardware. Printers, scanners, mouse and keyboard are considered hardware.

Software/Programs

Software are things you can buy or install that does a specific task. For example, your word processor like Microsoft Word, Excel, and PowerPoint are programs designed to create documents, spreadsheets or presentations. Microsoft's Internet Explorer® are programs designed that allows you to get onto and browse the Internet.

Microsoft Outlook are programs designed for you to create and send e-mail. Norton Antivirus, AVG and McAfee are programs designed to protect your computer from viruses and malware, which are also programs designed to try to take control your computer or worse, look for information to steal your identity among other things.

Note – You need hardware and software working together to make your computer work. Just having one without the other is like having a car with no gas in it.

Malware

Malware is software designed to take over your computer without your consent. Malware comes in many forms such as:

- Adware/Spyware – Adware/Spyware is any program that is supported by advertisements that flash within the program itself. These programs often track your internet surfing habits and cater the ads according to the types of other WebPages you visit and bombard you with pop-up ads and or e-mails about various products among other things such as changing computer settings, installing additional programs, such as key loggers, slow internet connections and Browser Hijacking which is explained next.

- Browser Hijacking – Browser hijacking is a common online attack designed to take over a computers web browser and change how and what it displays when you're surfing the Web.

- Key loggers – Key loggers are programs designed to record what you type into your computer with your keyboard. Key loggers can be used to try to track passwords and other information someone would use to go into your e-mail or online banking websites. That information can be sent back to owners of the malicious programs for identity theft or any other type of online crime.

- Toolbars – Toolbars are programs that plug into web browsers that provide enhanced functionality. Google and the Yahoo Toolbars are legitimate toolbars, but malicious toolbars can be also installed by programs that gather personal data and use that data for many online crimes.

Note – It is very important to be careful with what you or other people using your computer download and install from the Internet because it has become very easy to install these types of programs on your computer and put yourself at risk for any of the above items mentioned about viruses and malware. I will explain in detail how to protect you from these bad programs in Chapter Six and Seven.

Hard Drive/Hard Disk

The hard drive is an actual part inside the computer that information is saved to. We can refer the Hard drive (Usually the C: drive in the My Computer Section) as a file cabinet that everything is stored. Inside the file cabinet are files and folders that represent our things. We would organize our files in folders so that it would be easier to pull out the things we want to see. The same thing goes in computers. Within our file cabinet, there is a folder called My Documents, My Pictures, My Music. Ideally we would create folders within these folders to identify what is inside them.

There are removable or portable hard drives which you can plug into the computer and remove from the computer for additional storage, but I would only recommend these for backup purposes. I would fully explain this and the reasons for backing up your computer in Chapter Five: The Critical Task of Backing up Your Computer.

Ram/Memory

Memory could best be described as short-term storage of the computer. It is where information is stored for short periods of time. That is why it is very important to save your work constantly just in case of a glitch happening with the computer causing it to restart or freeze up because it is only there until the computer turns off, then it is gone forever. Of course the more you have of this, the better.

The way that a computer uses the hard disk and memory to operate can best be described as this. We remember quickly what we had done yesterday, but if we are asked about things that happened last year, we would have to think harder (Referring to our brains "Hard Drive" to remember things that happened a while ago and recall it into memory) This is basically how information is exchanged in the computer. The computer takes information from the Hard Drive and loads it into its memory so that it could be worked with or remembered quickly.

Operating System

The operating system is the most critical piece of software for your computer. It is the "Master Program". Without it, your computer will simply not operate at all. It controls everything on your computer. It provides a mean for you to actually use your computer by providing a bridge between you and all of your installed or connected hardware. The Operating System is the base for the software that is installed on your system. There are several operating systems out there for computers. Microsoft Windows® is an operating system. This operating system is the focus of this book. Linux is another operating system that is available for computers. Macintoshes have an operating system called Mac® OS X.

Mouse

The mouse is the hardware device that is connected to your computer that looks like a flattened egg that controls the cursor on the screen. You use this device by sliding it across a "Mouse pad" or any other surface on your desk or table. The mouse has 2 buttons for clicking to perform an action. You can either "Left Click" or you can "Right Click". A picture of a mouse with which buttons are the Left or Right Click is shown below:

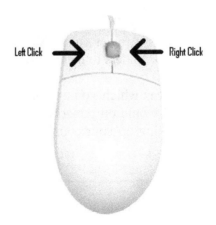

Left Click → ← Right Click

Cursor

A cursor is one of two things. A cursor can be an arrow or another shaped object that moves around the screen when you move your mouse around. It acts like a pointer on the screen so that you can perform an action by Left or Right Clicking your mouse. Also a cursor can be the blinking vertical line in programs such as word processors to indicate where you are typing.

Double and Single Clicking

A Double Click is an act where you press the left side of the mouse down quickly twice without moving the mouse at all. A single click is the act of pressing down the left side of the mouse once without moving the mouse at all.

Keyboard

Keyboards are hardware devices that have different letters on keys that allow you to type.

Printer

Printers are hardware devices that perform duplication or prints.

Scanner

A Scanner is a hardware device that is connected to your computer that allows you to import items into your computer such as pictures that you have or documents that you want to save, e-mail, duplicate or archive digitally.

Icon

Icons are small pictures on your screen that represent many things. On your desktop (The main screen on the computer), Icons represent programs installed on your computer. You would left double-click the picture to start that particular program. Throughout this book, you will see that Icons can represent things you can do within certain programs also. Like in a word document, you can have a menu with many icons on them that can represent sending to print to saving a document.

PC

This term is short for "Personal Computer". A personal computer is a computer designed to be used by one person at a time. At its core meaning, "PC" Refers to computers originally made by IBM. Nowadays, the term "PC" has been redefined considerably due to the fact that there are many companies making PC's such as Dell, HP and Toshiba to name a few.

Mac/Macintosh

This is a type of personal computer manufactured by Apple® Corporation. The Macintosh was the first computer to feature a mouse, icons and cursors to use the computer. Macintoshes are mainly used for Professional Photo, Music and Video Editing.

USB Port

The USB Ports are where you can plug in various devices. It is a very versatile type of connection because many hardware devices are being made to use these ports from Printers and Scanners, Digital Cameras, to Flash Drives. A picture showing what a USB Port looks like is shown below.

Flash/Jump Drives

Flash/Jump drives are one of many types of removable storage. These devices are plugged into one of the USB Ports. Files, Pictures and other things can be saved to this device. These are now being used in place of floppy disks. A picture of what a Flash/Jump drive looks like is shown below.

CPU/Processor

The CPU/Processor is the "Brain" of the computer. It is the part of the computer that does all of the thinking for the computer.

Gigabyte

Gigabyte is a unit of computer memory or data storage capacity equal to 1,024 megabytes. The term Gigabyte can refer to both computer Hard Drives and Computer Memory. You can tell the difference about which gigabyte it is by knowing that the computer memory is always referred by the smaller number and the computer hard drive space is referred to the larger number.

Like I had said earlier in this chapter, these computer terms or definitions are not all of the terms we talk about when we geeks discuss computers. Not by a long shot. Most other terms are out of the scope of this particular book. But the above translations of the "Computer Lingo" are all of the terminologies that you need to know to effectively be knowledgeable and comfortable operating a computer. I hope that I did not put you to sleep with all of this computer terminology and their meanings. But it is necessary to be able to follow along with the rest of this book.

The next chapter of this book goes into the fun stuff. Getting into and actually working with your computer, which is the main reason why you purchased this book! With no further delays, let's proceed to Chapter Two: Getting Acquainted with the Desktop and Microsoft Windows®.

How To Turn Your Computer On

The first thing that has to be done before we can start working with Windows is to turn your computer on. Every computer or laptop is made differently and computer manufacturers place the power button in many different places on the computer or laptop. But the one thing you need to keep in mind is that on every computer, the power button has an icon that looks like the picture below:

To turn your computer on, find the button that has the icon that looks like the picture shown above and press that button. On a desktop computer, you will find the same icon on your monitor power button also. Press the button to turn your monitor on.

How To Turn Your Computer Off (Shut Down)

To turn your computer off, you have to start a process called shutting down. The process of shutting down makes sure that the computer turns off programs and the many parts of your computer properly. To shut down your computer depends on which operating system you are using.

To Shut Down A Computer Using Windows 7:

Move your mouse cursor down to the lower left part of your screen and single left click the start menu button. It looks like this ⊞ the start menu will come up. It will look like the picture shown below. On the lower right part of the start menu, there will be a button that says "Shut Down". It will look like the picture shown below:

Single left click on it. After you click on it, your computer will then shutdown and turn off by itself.

Chapter Two:

Getting Acquainted With The Desktop And Microsoft Windows®

Chapter Two: Getting Acquainted with the Desktop And Microsoft Windows®.

After you setup your computer and turned it on, your computer will do a quick hardware check. After that check has completed, the computer goes to the hard drive and start that "Master Program" called the operating system. That process is called booting up. The booting up process is the act of the computer setting up everything it needs to operate the computer at all. Once Windows has fully booted up, it will go right to the desktop screen where you can start using your computer. The pictures below are what the desktop looks like for Windows 7

Windows 7® Desktop

Your Windows desktop has several parts to it. The first part that we are going to talk about is located at the bottom of the desktop called the "Task Bar". The picture below shows what the task bar looks like for Windows 7®. The task bar itself has several parts to it. First, we are going to talk about the Start Menu.

Windows 7® Task Bar

In the Windows 7® task bar, you have the Windows logo representing the start menu. The start menu allows us to access all that the computer has to offer including our programs, saved documents and pictures, and all of our computer settings. Grab your mouse and move your cursor down to the lower left part of the taskbar and single left click on the Windows logo to show the start menu.

When you single left click the Windows logo to show the start menu, it should look like the following picture below.

Windows 7® Start Menu

At the top right part of the start menu, you will find the name of the current user logged onto the computer. In the Windows 7® screen, it is my name, Reginald Prior. In the start menu, there are two areas. The left side contains three separate areas. On the top third of the left side of the menu, you have the Icons for the programs that you use often on this computer.

Microsoft added this feature because it makes it convenient to have quicker access to the programs you use the most. To gain access to all of the other programs that are installed on the computer, the second third of the left side of the start menu has the "All Programs" option where you single left-click on that option, a menu shows up with all of the programs that you have installed on your computer like the next picture shows.

The third part of the Start menu is the integrated search feature. I will explain this section in detail in the "Searching For Things On Your Computer" section later in this book. On the right side of the start menu, there are icons to access different parts of Microsoft Windows® that are most used such as:

- Documents – The default place where word processors saves files you want to keep for future retrieval

- Pictures - The default place where image programs and or scanning software saves pictures you want to keep for future retrieval

- Music - The default place where music programs saves music files you want to keep for future retrieval

- Games – This is where the standard games that comes with Windows are located at including the ever popular game, Solitaire

- Devices and Printers – Devices and Printers gives you a quick view and access of all of your connected and wireless devices on your computer in one place. By viewing the contents of this folder, you can check to see which devices you have connected, view details about the devices, and learn what tasks you can perform with them by right clicking on the device and selecting the task you would like to do.

- Computer – Computer is where you can explore the contents of your computer drives as well as manage the files on your computer. The picture below shows what the Computer window looks like in Windows 7® .

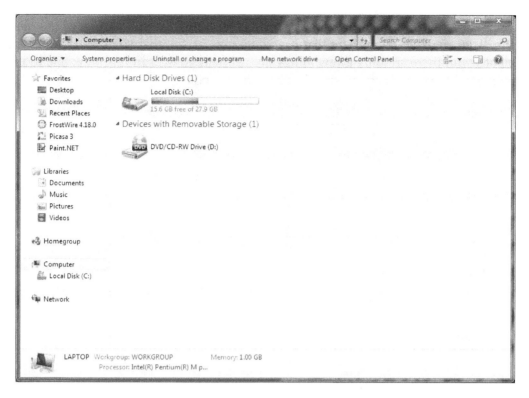

Windows 7® Computer Window

In the Computer menu, you see icons that represents the hard drive (Local Disk C :), CD or DVD Drives and other things such as scanners, etc.

- Control Panel – This is where all of the settings for Windows are located at. The Control Panel is shown in the picture below:

As you can see, the Control Panel at first glance can be very intimidating because of the many options available here. True there are things here that if you are not careful, that you can do some real damage to your computer. But there are only a few things that we will go over in this book due to the fact that many things in the control panel are outside the scope of this book.

What we are going to be concerned with is going over how to change how your desktop looks like, setting up/changing a screen saver, adding or removing users that are allowed to use the computer, and adjusting the date or time on the computer. Keep in mind that when you're in doubt about anything in the control panel, don't change any settings at all. You are better safe than sorry. We will now go over how to change what your desktop looks like.

<u>Changing The Background Of Your Desktop</u>

When you take a first glance at the Windows 7 Desktop, you are looking at the "Default" desktop background screen. The first thing most people would do with their desktop is to change the desktop picture so their personal computer would become more "personal". The first step to personalizing your desktop is to go to the control panel.

To get to the control panel, move your mouse cursor to the start menu , and single left click on it. Single left click on the control panel option. Within the control panel, the option to change your background of your desktop is available by double left clicking on the "Personalization" option. The menu that comes up should look like the following screen shown below.

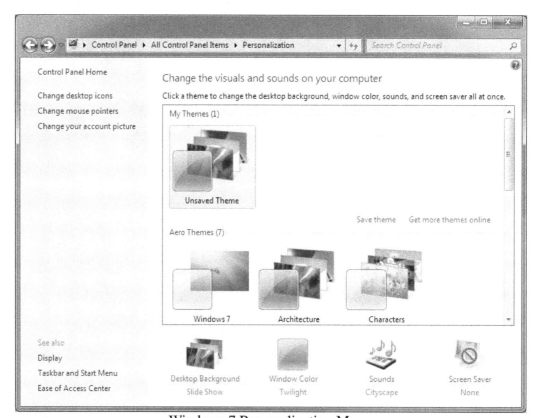

Windows 7 Personalization Menu

Note – One of the new changes in Windows 7®, is now the background pictures are now packaged in "Themes". Themes are a feature in Windows 7 to keep the desktop looking fresh and dynamic and also be like an active screensaver. You can create your own themes from pictures that you may have downloaded into the "Pictures" folder. Also, you can customize your computer by changing the window color or the sound themes. I will go over all of these things in detail later in the section "Creating Custom Themes"

To change the current theme in Windows 7®, move your mouse cursor to any one of the themes listed in this window that looks interesting to you and single left click on it. Windows will change the screen, window color and the sound scheme temporarily. Once you found the theme you like, you can exit the menu by just moving your mouse cursor to the red "X" and single-left click on it at the top-right part of the current window. It should look like this ▭ ▢ ✕ . You can create custom themes, which I will explain in detail in the next section of this book.

Creating Custom Themes

You can customize any theme by selecting any one of the further customization options listed at the bottom of the "Personalization" menu window. You get to the personalization window in the control panel by moving your mouse cursor to the start menu, and single left clicking on it. Then single left click on the control panel option. Within the control panel, the option to change your background of your desktop is available by double left clicking on the "Personalization" option. First you will single left click on a current theme that you would like to customize. Windows will then change the theme to the one you had just selected.

At the bottom of the personalization menu screen, you will see additional options to further customize the theme as shown in the picture shown below:

| Desktop Background | Window Color | Sounds | Screen Saver |
| Slide Show | Twilight | Cityscape | None |

Each one of these options allows you to further change the current theme colors, and background pictures among other things to create your own personalized theme. In this section:

23

If you select:

Desktop Background –

The Desktop Background menu will come up like the picture shown below:

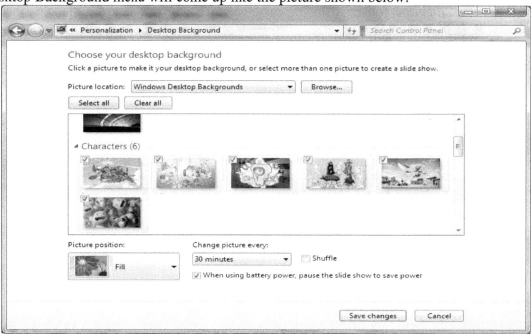

In this section, you have the option of selecting how the theme picture is shown on the screen with the picture position drop down menu, also what pictures you want to actually to have show in this theme. You can check and uncheck individual pictures shown in this menu by moving your mouse cursor to the top left side of the checkbox next to the picture and single left click on it to uncheck or check it.

To import your own pictures into this theme for showing on your desktop, move your mouse cursor to the picture location drop menu, single left click on it and select the "Pictures Library" option. That will load the pictures that you have saved in the "Pictures" folder and make them available to load into the theme. To have a particular picture checked, the picture will show in the theme, and having a picture unchecked means that the picture will not show in the current theme.

The second thing you can do to customize a theme is to have your pictures arranged a certain way on the screen when the theme shows on the screen. Single left click the drop menu under the "Picture Position" area of this window, you will see several options on how to arrange the desktop picture on the screen. The list of the options and a brief explanation is listed below:

Here's an explanation of the three options of how you can have the picture arranged on your desktop:

- Centered – The picture will appear in the center of the screen with the pictures real size.
- Tile – The picture will appear with as many images as necessary to fill the screen shown like tiles on a kitchen floor.
- Stretch – The picture will appear once, stretching it to fill up the whole screen.

As you will notice in the area where all of the pictures are, there are more pictures there than what is shown currently. To the right of the window is what we call "Slider Bars". Here's s picture of what they look like.

Windows 7® Slider Bar

If you had wanted to see more pictures than what initially shows in the menu, move your mouse cursor to the middle part of the slider bar where the actual slider is, single left click and hold the button down, move your mouse up and down to show more things in the menu or single left click on the up or down arrows to move the menu up or down. In most programs or "Windows" in Windows, you will see these same sliders indicating that is more in the current program or window than what is showing currently.

Once the desired position layout has been selected, single left click the "save changes" button in the menu and the desired changes will take place.

<u>Window Color –</u>

This option allows you to change the color that your windows, Start menu and taskbar will look like. The Window Color option comes up like the picture shown below:

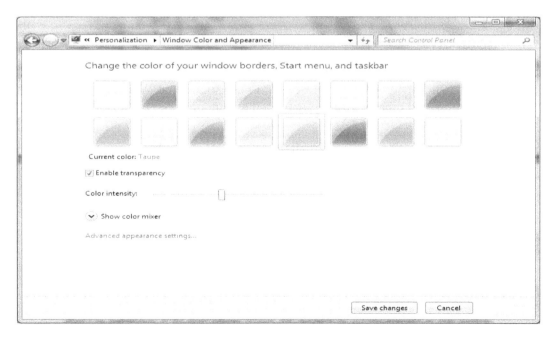

For example, this window shows that the current color of this window is Taupe. If you move your mouse cursor and single left click on the red color in this menu, the color of the current window, start menu and the taskbar will change to the red color (Which is called Ruby in this case) as shown in the picture below:

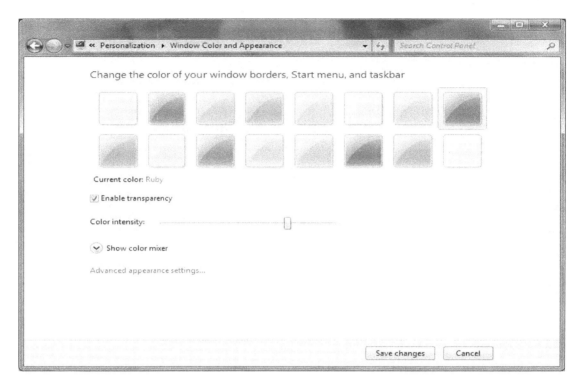

When you are satisfied about the color of your theme, move your mouse cursor and single left click on the "Save Changes" button and your desired theme color will be saved, and the main personalization menu will come back up.

Sounds -

The sounds menu allows you to select which determine many things that happens in windows from the sound that the computer makes when an error occurs, to the sound that Windows makes when you are logging into the computer, and other various events on the computer.

To get to the sounds menu, within the "personalization" menu, at the bottom of the window, you will see the option where you can single left click on the "Sounds" icon and go to the sounds menu as shown in the picture on the next page:

To change a sound scheme, move your mouse cursor to the "Sound Scheme" drop down menu, single left click on the sound scheme drop box, select a scheme in the drop menu, single left click to select the theme. In the box below that drop menu, are the individual events that you can assign sounds to. where there is a little speaker icon like this , you can single left click on that particular event, move your mouse cursor and single left click the "Test" button to preview what that sound setting would sound like.

You can change the sound by single left clicking on the Sounds drop menu below the Program Events section of this menu. A menu with more available sounds will come up. Single left click on any one of them and move your mouse cursor to the Test button and single left click on it to preview that particular sound. If you like the particular sound for that event, then single left click on the "Apply" button. When finished customizing the sound schemes, move your mouse cursor to the "OK" button and single left click on it, or if you don't want to make any changes to the sound scheme, then single left click on the "Cancel" Button.

Screen Saver -

The screen saver menu allows you to change the screen saver on your computer. Screen savers were created to prevent monitor burn-in ghost images, which permenently damages the monitor. I will go over in detail on how to change your screensaver in the "Changing Your Screensaver" section later in this book.

After you have tweaked all of the personalization settings and created your ideal theme, it will show up in the personalization menu under the "My Themes" section as being called "Unsaved Theme". You can save the theme under another name by moving your mouse cursor to the theme, right click on the theme and single left click on the "Save Theme" menu choice. A pop up box will come up asking you to type a name in for the name of the theme as shown in the picture below:

Type a name for this theme, and single left click on the save button. Your new customized theme will be saved under that name for easy identification.

Sharing Your Custom Windows 7 Themes With Friends & Family

Another new thing that is new and exclusive with Windows 7 is that when you get through creating your perfect theme, you can send it to all of your friends and family that are running Windows 7 and they can enjoy your customized theme on their computer also!

To prepare your custom theme for sharing with your friends and family, first go to the personalization menu in the control panel. To get to the control panel, move your mouse cursor to the start menu, then single left click on the control panel option. Within the control panel, the option to change your background of your desktop is available by double left clicking on the "Personalization" option. The menu that comes up should look like the following screen shown below:

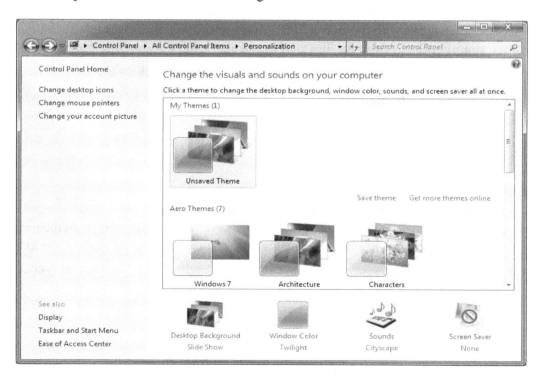

Under the "My Themes" section of the personalization menu, you will have listed all of your custom themes that you have saved. To send it to other people, you have to "package" the theme. To package the theme, move your mouse cursor to the desired theme to send, and single right click on it. A menu will come up. Single left click on the "Save Theme For Sharing" menu option. A menu box will come up as shown in the picture shown below asking you what name you want to save the "Packaged" theme as.

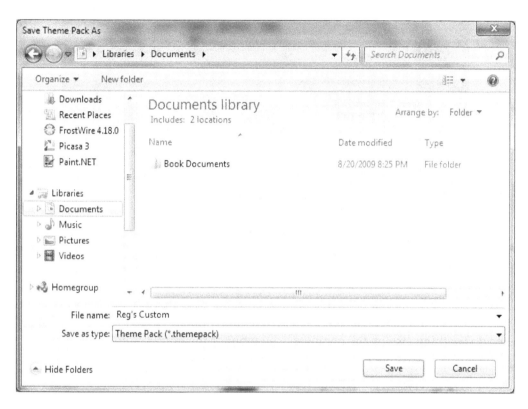

Type a name in the file name textbox and single left click on the "Save" button. Your theme will be packaged for sending via E-Mail or however you wish to give your customized theme to other people.

Changing/Configuring Your Screensaver

When you're working on your computer and the phone rings, or any situation happens where you have to leave your computer for some period of time. There is nothing wrong with this practice in general; as it saves time on when you have to come back to work on your computer. Well, back in the eighties and early nineties, people would leave their computer for a long time and have the same program on their screen.

But what was happening was a process was happening called burn-in, which is a shadowing or ghosting of a image on the screen. You could be working on another program, but see a ghost image of the program in the screen that you or another person was looking at for long periods of time. The picture shown shows an example of what a monitor burn-in image looks like.

Screensavers were then created to resolve this issue by showing different images on the screen to prevent monitor burn-in, in which permanently damages the monitor.

To change/configure a screensaver, single left click the start menu and single left click on control panel. In the control panel, double left click on the "Personalization" Option and single left click the "Screen Saver" button at the bottom of that menu. Your screen should look like the picture shown below:

Note – Most new computer monitors have a "Power Save" setting that if the monitor detects no activity happening on the screen after some period of time, then the monitor shuts itself down. But if you move your mouse or do anything else on the computer, the monitor then turns itself back on.

From the drop list in either Windows 7®, move your mouse cursor to the section where it says "Screen Saver" with what we call a "Drop Menu" and single left click on the down arrow to show all of the screen savers in the drop menu.

Choose one from the drop list by single left clicking on one of the choices. A small preview is shown in the small monitor screen above. If you want to see how the screensaver looks like on the screen before making it a final decision, single left click the "Preview" button in the window and the screensaver comes up full screen. To get out of preview mode, just move the mouse around and it should go back to the screensaver menu.

You can modify the time the computer waits before the computer starts the screensaver by typing in a number that would represent the amount of minutes in the box below the drop menu for the selection of screensavers. When you are satisfied with choosing the screensaver and amount of time the computer waits before starting the screensaver, single left click the OK button. Now your screensaver is all setup and ready to go!

Searching For Things On Your Computer

The last section that we're going to cover from the start menu is one of the more important parts. Especially if you have a tendency to forget where things were saved, is search feature. Computers today hold a great deal of information. because of this, I strongly suggest when you are working on anything on your computer that you save them to the "Documents", "Pictures" or "Music" Folders. Why do I suggest these three folders? I suggest these folders because for one, they are easily found from anywhere on the computer, and makes it simpler to backup the computer.

For example, if you were working on an important presentation, saved it on the computer, but forgot where on the computer it was saved, the search feature can help you out. In Windows 7®, Microsoft changed the way you search for files by integrating the search in the start menu itself. You search for files in Windows 7® by single left clicking on the start menu, type the phrase or words you want to search for in the search box on the start menu. It looks like the picture below:

After you type in the phrase in the search box, single left click the search button ▣, the search will start. The search results will show in the start menu itself, as shown in the picture shown:

These past sections had explained the start menu and the options grouped together. The start menu makes it easier to use your computer.

The Shortcuts/Open Programs Area Of The Windows Toolbar

The shortcuts area is the section right of the start menu where you access particular programs quickly. The icons that are on the shortcuts area are:

- This represents Microsoft's Internet Explorer®. This program is used to access the Internet

- This represents Windows Explorer. This is used to access your files and folders.

The open programs area is the section next to the shortcut area where we can see buttons that represents programs, menu items or folders that are currently open on the computer.

A new feature with Windows 7 on the open programs area of the bottom toolbar is a nice feature called Taskbar Preview. This feature allows you to have many programs open at the same time without cluttering your taskbar with multiple icons of the same program with different files that you may be currently working on. If for example, you have multiple files open in Paint in either Windows XP, there used to be a icon for each file open on the open programs taskbar as shown in the next picture:

As you can see, if I was working on many different things at the same time in Paint, and needed to go back and forth between documents, it will become more difficult to see exactly which file is which due to the cluttered nature of the taskbar. What Microsoft has made it so that files that you may be working on in the same program are grouped together in stacks as shown in the picture below:

But they also resolved the frustration of not being able to know what you had currently open by adding preview windows. Whenever you move your mouse cursor over a icon on the taskbar, If anything is currently open in that program, a preview window will appear showing a preview of everything that you have open in that particular program. In the pictures shown below, you can see what the preview window would look like with one thing open in a program, and when there multiple things open in a program.

Single Preview Window

Multiple Files Preview Windows

If you move your mouse cursor over the preview window, you can either do one of two things. If you want to close a particular file or program, you can single left click on the red "X" that will appear in the preview window and that particular file or program will close. Or if you want to bring it back to full screen to continue working on it, single left click the desired window and whatever you were working on in that program will come back up on the screen for you.

Using The New Windows 7 Jump Lists Feature

The Windows 7 Jump Lists feature is designed to provide you quick access to documents and other tasks associated with your applications. You can think of Jump Lists like little application-specific Start menus. Jump Lists can be found on the application icons that appear on the Taskbar when an application is running or on the Start menu in the recently opened programs section. Jump Lists can also be found on the icons of applications that have been specifically *pinned* to the Taskbar or the Start menu.

Windows 7 Taskbar

To view a jump list for a specific program, move your mouse cursor to any program icon on the taskbar, and single right click on it. In this case, I will single right click on the Internet Explorer icon, which looks like this 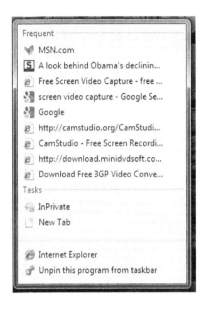 A pop up menu showing the jump list will show on the screen as shown in the picture below:

In this jump list, this shows all of the recent websites that have recently been visited and also other tasks that you can do in Internet Explorer such as single left clicking on the "New Tab" option that would open up Internet Explorer with a blank tab for you to visit a website. That what jump lists are in a nutshell, A more quicker and more efficient way to use your programs that are on your computer.

Note- "Pinning" an application to the taskbar allows you to have shortcuts to your most used programs on the computer for easy access. To "Pin" an application, have your program open, Single right click on the application icon, the jump list for that application will pop up, and then single left click on the "Pin This Program To The Taskbar" option. The program will now have a shortcut on the Taskbar.

The Notification Area Of The Windows Toolbar

The notification area of the Windows Toolbar are icons to the far right that represent programs that starts up automatically when the computer boots up. Also displays alerts about when Microsoft releases updates to Windows, The new action area center alerts, Your internet connection and battery status (If you are working on a laptop) and the current time.

Notification Area Icon Meanings:

- This icon represents the Action Center that Microsoft has implemented in Windows 7. The Action Center is a single area that collects important notification messages about security and maintenance. When you single left click the Action Center, you'll see information about the things you need to take action on, and find helpful links to troubleshooters and other tools that can help fix problems.

- This icon represents the current power settings. If you are currently working on a desktop, the icon will turn into a monitor with an electric plug next to it. If your computer is a laptop and it is currently plugged in, the icon would be a battery with an electric plug next to it as such as the current picture. If the laptop is unplugged and running on battery, the battery icon would be showing by itself.

- This icon represents your current Internet connection status. If you are currently working on a desktop, the icon will show up like a computer monitor with the internet plug next to it. If you are on a laptop connected to a wireless internet connection, the icon will show up like the signal bars on your cellular phone as shown in the picture shown here.

- This icon represents the volume setting of the speakers on your computer. You can adjust the volume simply by moving your mouse cursor and single left clicking on it. A slider bar menu will appear representing the volume level. The picture shown below represents the volume level menu.

Move your mouse cursor to the actual slider, single left click and hold the button down while moving your mouse up or down to change the volume. When you reach the desired volume, just let go of the left mouse button.

- This icon represents the current time of the computer. You can change the date and time settings by single left clicking on this icon. I will explain this more in detail in the next section.

Changing The Time On Your Computer

On the far right of the Windows task bar notification area, there is the clock. If you move your cursor over the clock and leave the cursor there for a couple of seconds without clicking on anything, the full date will show as a mini popup. To change the time or date on the computer, single left click on the clock and single left click on "Change date and time settings link in Windows 7®, and the date and properties window will come up looking like the picture shown below:

Windows 7 Date and Time Settings Menu

In Windows 7®, single left click the "Change date and time" button. To change the date, select the desired month from the top of the calendar by single left clicking on the left or right arrow next to the month menu, and the month selection will change with each mouse click. Then when you have the desired month, then single left click on the desired date. Then single left click first on the "Apply" button and then the "OK" button.

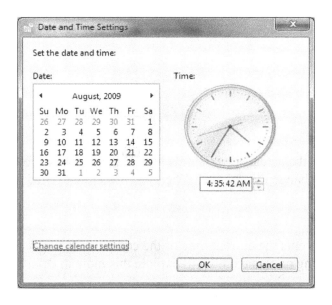

To change the time, move your mouse cursor over the section of time you want to change and single left click on it, type the number of the desired hour or minutes depending on which section of time you were changing. After you were done making desired changes to the date and time, single left click the "Apply" button and then single left click the "OK" button. Your date and time is now set.

Changing The Current Time Zone

In Windows 7®, to change the current time zone that you are currently in, single left click on the "Time Zone" button in the Date and Time window, select the desired time zone from the drop menu and single left clicking the "OK" button. Your desired time zone will be now set.

Using The Recycle Bin

The recycle bin is space reserved on the computer so that if you accidently hit the delete key and delete a file or folder, you can easily retrieve it. Deleting a file is a 2 step process on Windows. By default, the recycle bin can restore a file or folder back to the place it got deleted from. For example, if the file got deleted from the "Documents" folder, you could restore it back to the documents folder. The recycle bin keeps documents or folders there until it is permanently "emptied" from the recycle bin. Then the file or folder is gone forever.

To open the recycle bin, double left click on the recycle bin icon on the desktop. The recycle bin window will then come up looking like the picture shown below:

Windows 7® Recycle Bin

To put things in the recycle bin, single left click on the file or folder you want to have removed from the computer and hit the "Delete" key on the keyboard. Windows will ask you the question "Are you sure you want to send this file to the Recycle Bin?" with 2 buttons saying yes or no. If you select no, nothing happens. If you single left click yes, the files will be sent to the recycle bin.

To restore a file or folder, move your cursor to the desired file in the recycle bin to be restored; single left-click on it, Then single left click the "Restore the selected item" button at the top of the window. The file or folder will be taken out of the recycle bin and placed back to the place it was before on the computer.

To empty the recycle bin (Remember, after you empty the recycle bin, everything that is here is GONE FOREVER!), single left click the "Empty The Recycle Bin" button. Windows will ask you the question "Are you sure you want to delete" and with 2 buttons saying yes or no. If you select no, nothing happens. If you select yes, then the files will be deleted.

Adding/Changing Users In Windows

Do you have more than one person that will be using your computer? Do you want to keep your documents and other files separate from the other person(s) that will be using your computer and vice versa? In this section, you will learn how to add/change users to Windows. Adding users is a great way to keep your personal files separate while still having the ability to share programs.

First, open the Control Panel by single left clicking on the Start Button, then single left click on the Control Panel icon. In the Control Panel, scroll down to the Users Accounts Icon and single left click it.

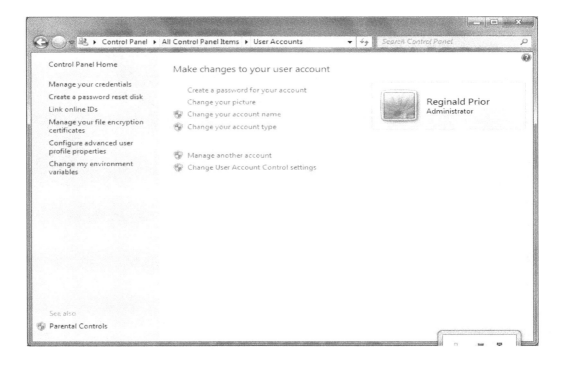

With the Users Accounts window open, single left click on the "Manage another Account" option. The window should come up like the picture shown on the next page:

Move your mouse cursor and single left click on the "Create a new account" link in this menu. Enter the name of the new user in the box provided and then single left click on the next button.

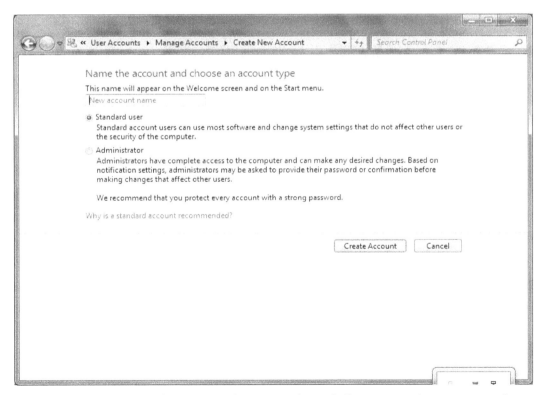

Next, choose the account type. If you want the user to have full access to the computer, then you need to choose the Computer Administrator option. If you want the user to have limited access to the computer, meaning that the new user cannot just install any kind of programs without restrictions, you should choose the limited option. I recommend using the limited option; however, most people will use the administrator option. When finished, single left click the Create Account button.

You will return to the User Accounts window and you should now see your new user's icon.

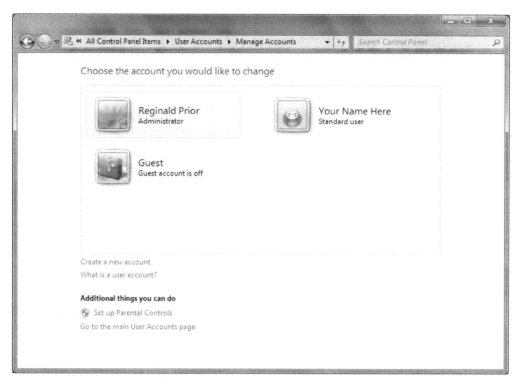

<u>Changing User Account Type</u>

If you want to make changes to an account that is already on this computer, move your mouse cursor to the account you want to change and single left click on it. You can change or create a account password among other things. Single left click on the "Change the account type" link.

Account Type Meanings:

Administrator	Limited Account Access
This type of user has the ability to install, remove and change any of the settings on the computer, in other words, full unrestricted access to the computer.	This user can use the programs installed on the computer, but cannot change any settings. This setting is perfect for anybody outside of yourself using this computer.

Single left click on the button of which type of account you wish this user to have and then single left click on the "Change Account Type" button. The account type settings has now been changed.

Reading Windows Pathnames

Every file on your computer has a pathname. A pathname is in short, is the exact location of a file on your computer. You might be asking yourself, how do I find the pathname of a file on my computer? Well the pathname is near the top of the current window that you have open. The picture below shows exactly where the pathname usually is located in a window.

Say for instance your budget that you typed out on a word processor is located at

C:\Users\Reginald Prior\document.doc?

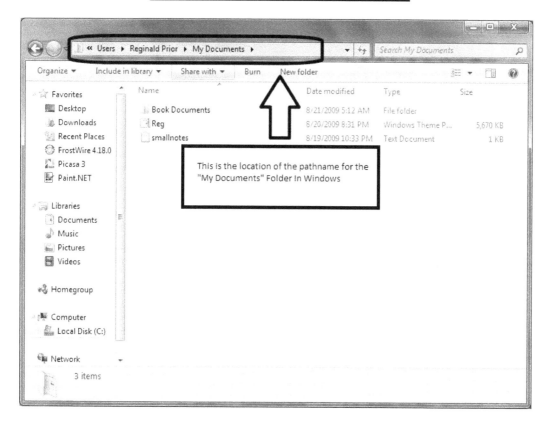

How would you decipher exactly on your computer where this file is located? Well, I am about to explain how to go straight to this document. Remember how I told you in chapter one the C: drive was like a file cabinet? And how things inside the file cabinet were organized by files inside folders? Well, files on computers are organized the same way.

First, move your mouse cursor and single left click on the start menu, then move your mouse cursor and single left click on the "Computer" menu. Your "Computer" window will come up. Then move your mouse cursor to the Local Disk C: icon 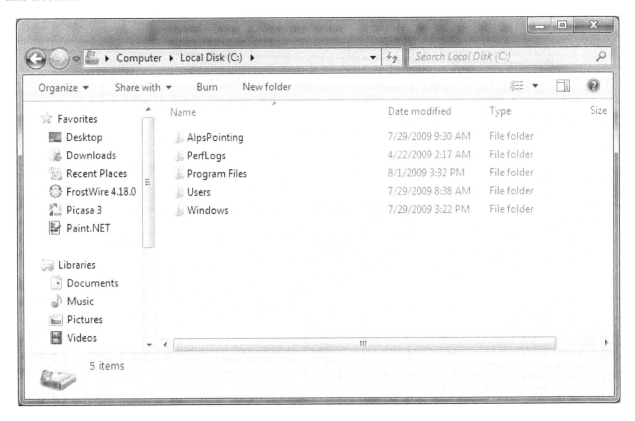 and double left click on it. That takes care of the C:\ part of the pathname. Look in that window for the "Users" Folder. It will actually look like a folder.

Double left click on that folder. In that folder, another folder in this case should represent the current user on the computer. In this example, it is my name, so double left click on this folder.

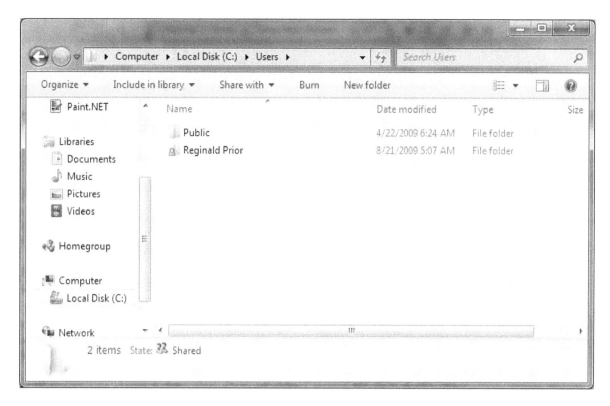

In this folder, you should see the document.doc file that you are originally looking for. That's in a nutshell is how you would read a pathname.

This concludes chapter two on getting to know the Windows desktop and the many features available in Windows. Hopefully up to this part in the book, you should feel comfortable working on your computer and explore in confidence on the other inner workings of Windows. We proceed now to Chapter Three: Basic Internet Browsing.

Chapter Three:

Basic Internet Browsing

Chapter Three: Basic Internet Browsing

The Internet is many things to many people. People use the Internet for things such as finding shopping deals and travel fares. Some people use the Internet for news and information. Other people use the Internet to express themselves through blogs (Online Diaries), Video Sites (YouTube) or Social Networking websites (MySpace, Face book, Twitter).

People use the Internet for malicious acts also. I will explain that in more detail in Chapter Six: Computer Maintenance and Upkeep. This chapter is concerned about getting you confident to discover the many millions of websites on the Internet and to make sense of using the Internet and using web browsers.

In chapter one, we explained what a web browser is. A web browser is a program that allows you to easily navigate the internet. So how do you get connected to the internet? Well, first and foremost, you have to sign up with an internet service provider or ISP. Your internet service provider could be your local cable or Telephone Company, or a national Wi-Fi internet carrier such as Verizon or AT&T. There are also dial-up services that you can sign up with such as AOL, but the price of high-speed internet has gone down to being very affordable, does not tie up your phone line and dramatically faster, it will be worth getting a high speed line installed.

After you have signed up with an internet service provider and have them come out to your home and setup the service, you are ready to go. If you already have internet service, then we are ready for the next step, opening up your web browser. In Windows, you already have a web browser installed on your computer called Microsoft's Internet Explorer®.

On your desktop or your taskbar, you will find an icon that looks like this ![icon] . Single left click on this logo and Microsoft's Internet Explorer® comes up and load the default website that has been programmed into the program. You can change this webpage if you like, but will go over this later in this chapter.

Microsoft Microsoft's Internet Explorer® 8

Before we go into the sections of your web browser to surf the internet, there is more "Computer Lingo" that describes things on the internet. Don't worry; this list is not as long as the list in chapter one talking about computers in general. These and many more terms can be found at http://www.netlingo.com.

Email -- (Electronic Mail) Messages, usually text, sent from one person to another via computer

Hyperlink / Link - The text or graphics on a Web site that can be clicked on with a mouse to take you to another website or a different area of the same Web page.

Download - To transfer a file or files from one computer to another.

E-Commerce - Simply put, it means conducting business online

Encryption - The process of protecting information as it moves from one computer to another

ISP - A company that provides user's access to the Internet.

Username- The name you use to access certain programs, Web sites, software, or networks.

Login / Log In - The act of connecting to or accessing a remote computer system, network, or server

Netiquette - The code of conduct and unofficial rules that govern online interaction and behavior

Password - A combination of letters and other symbols needed to login to a computer system.

Phishing - An online scam in which the perpetrator sends out a large number of legitimate looking e-mails that appear to come from respected companies (such as Citibank, eBay, PayPal, MSN, Amazon.com, Yahoo, Best Buy, AOL, etc.) with the intent of "fishing" for personal and financial information from the recipient. These e-mails are falsely claiming to be the respected company who needs the user's information to update their files, when in fact, it is an attempt to scam the user into surrendering private information that will later be used for identity theft.

The phony e-mail directs the user to go to a Web site with the logo of the respected company, where they are asked to update personal information (such as passwords and credit cards, social security numbers, and bank account numbers) which the legitimate organization already has. The Web site, however, is bogus and has been established only to steal the users' information. The e-mail usually includes a threat stating the user's account will close if they do not receive this updated information in a specified time period.

Search Engine - A Web site (actually a program) that acts as a card catalog for the Internet.

Webmail - Webmail allows you to access your E-Mail on a Web page, using your web browser. This means you can read, send, and organize your e-mail on any computer, anywhere in the world, with an Internet connection. Webmail for an example are services such as Gmail, yahoo, or hotmail to name a few. Your ISP can also have a webmail service so that you can look at their email from anywhere on the Internet.

Getting Connected To Wireless Internet Hot Spots

If you are on a laptop or have a wireless network card installed on your computer, you have the ability to connect to wireless internet "Hot Spots". Hot Spots are areas which an <u>access point</u> provides public wireless internet to mobile visitors. Hotspots are often located in heavily populated places such as airports, train stations, libraries, marinas, conventions centers and hotels. Hotspots typically have a short range of access.

To view and connect to available hot spots, you need to know some information about them. First of all, there are two types of hot spots. The two types are:

1. **Protected or Secured** - These hot spots are password enabled (More Secure) so that users that know the password can access that particular hot spot. For example, if you are staying in a hotel and they provide internet access for guests, usually they password protect their access points so that non guests cannot access their internet connection. So you would have to get the password information from the front desk so that you can setup your computer to use the internet.

2. **Unsecure** – These hot sports are just that, unsecure. They don't require a password to be able to connect to them. You would just click on that hot spot and the computer will connect to it for Internet.

To view any available hot spots in range of your computer, move your cursor to the Internet Connection Status Icon on the start menu toolbar. It will look like this ▊▊ . Single left click on it and all of the Hot Spots within the range of this computer will show in the pop up menu. This looks like the picture shown below:

In the picture shown on the previous page, you see three available access points to connect to the Internet. Two of them are protected access points and one is unprotected. The unprotected access points will have yellow caution icons that look like this ▊▊ and the protected access points do not.

48

Move your mouse cursor to the access point that you want to connect to and single left click on it. In this case, I will connect to the "rplan" access point. Since this is a protected access point, the password prompt will come up asking for the password as shown in the picture shown below:

Type in the password for the hot spot and move your mouse cursor to the OK button and single left click on it. The computer will then connect to the access point for you to surf the Internet. That's how you connect to wireless hot spots.

Parts Of Your Web Browser

So let's go over the many parts of your web browser so that you will be able to surf the internet. The top section of the web browser contains 99% of what you will need to be able to surf the internet.

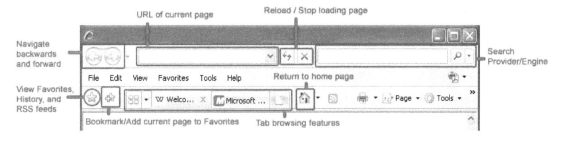

Top Part Of Microsoft's Internet Explorer® 8

The picture above shows the top section of Microsoft's Internet Explorer® 8. Many browsers share the same features. So let get started by going over the features and exactly what they mean.

Navigate Backwards And Forward – If you are looking at multiple websites, come upon a webpage, but quickly clicked on another link. But if want to go back to look at that previous webpage, the left arrow key will take you back to the previous webpage you were looking at, the right arrow key will take you to the webpage that you were looking at before you clicked the left arrow key.

URL Of Current Page – Address of the current page being viewed. If this box shows http://www.yahoo.com, the yahoo website should be showing below. Every webpage has a unique URL or address. You can also type in a specific webpage into this box by moving your cursor to this box and single left click on the box. It should all highlight in blue. When it is highlighted, you can type in the desired webpage you want to go to starting with www. Desired website name here .com, org, net or gov.

Reload/Stop Loading Page - When displaying a webpage, your web browser downloads the webpage from the Internet onto your computer. Therefore if the webpage changes, you can update the webpage in your browser window by clicking the **Reload button** with the green arrows. If the webpage is taking too long to load for any reason, you can stop the webpage by clicking on the **Stop button** with the red X. Click on the Reload button to start the downloading process again from the beginning.

Search Provider/Engine – This section of the web browser makes it easy to enter words to send directly to search engines. That will be discussed later in this chapter.

Return To Home Page – You click on the "Home" button to return you back to the default web page that is set for the web browser.

Bookmark/Add Current Page To Favorites – Favorites and Bookmarks are websites that you visit often to be within easy reach. If you find yourself always going to say, www.cnn.com you can "Bookmark" the webpage and go to your bookmarks menu with your mouse and single left click on the bookmark and it will then go to that particular website that you had bookmarked saving you from constantly typing it into the URL Box.

Like I said at the beginning of this chapter, there are now millions, if not billions of websites on the internet that covers any interest you may have and many other things. So how do you discover let alone find all of these WebPages? We start by typing in what we are interested in seeing on the internet by going through a search engine. A search engine collects information from all the websites on the internet and puts them into a webpage where you will be able to search and find them.

Using Search Providers/ Engines To Find Things On The Internet

There are many search engines on the internet that allows you to find websites that may interest you. The most used search engines are:

- Google – www.google.com
- Yahoo – www.yahoo.com
- MSN (Microsoft Search) – www.msn.com

The following sections in this chapter use Google search located at www.google.com . I find that Google has the most current and accurate databases of websites, and has a very simplistic layout which is easier to read as per the picture shown on the next page:

Say for example that we were in the market to purchase a car and want to do some research on various models to make sure that we are getting not only the best deal, but we are getting the best car to suit our current needs and price range. We can search Google for a specific vehicle type or model, but in this case, we are going to type in the box "car reviews" just like it is shown in the next picture:

Single left click on the "Google Search" button and the results will show up like shown in the picture on the next page:

As you can see, a lot of results came back for just the term "Car Reviews". Just a note for you to keep in mind, usually the top 20 results are exactly you are searching for. You can go deeper in the search, but usually the deeper you go into the results of a results, the less likely that the particular results show what you are looking for in the first place. Move your mouse cursor to a link (Usually in Blue Letters) and single left click on what looks interesting that you want to check out, and you will be taken to that webpage.

Well, that is how you would use a search engine to look for various things on the internet. Please feel free to try the other search engines out there if you wish. Have fun discovering the many different things on the Internet.

Adding And Using Bookmarks/Favorites

Bookmarks/Favorites are a quick & easy way to remember websites that you visit often. The instructions below show you how to create and use them.

To create favorites in Microsoft's Internet Explorer®

1. Go to the webpage you want to bookmark.
2. Single left click on the **Add to Favorites icon** or go to the **Favorites** menu.
3. Then single left click on **Add to Favorites**.
4. Give the webpage a name (e.g. *American Revolution*) or keep its original name.
5. Click **Add**.

To view and use favorites in Microsoft's Internet Explorer®

1. In Microsoft's Internet Explorer®, single left click on the **View Favorites** button ⭐ and select **Favorites**. (Another option is to single left click on the **Favorites menu** in the main toolbar.)
2. From that list, single left click on the bookmark of the webpage you want to see.

In this chapter, we went over the meat and potatoes of surfing the Internet and being able to bookmark websites as we come across them. Don't be afraid to do different kinds of searches and discover things that are out there.

Changing Default Web Page When Your Web Browser Loads

When you double left click on Microsoft's Internet Explorer® and the program loads up, the first web page that comes up is what we call the default or your home page. More than likely, the web page that comes up first is not the one that you would like to first come up when you go onto the Internet. This section shows you how to change that default or home page to whatever website you want it to be.

To change the default or home page of your web browser to the website of your choice, either it be a news website such as cnn.com or anything else, open up your web browser of choice and get it to the default or home page.

Microsoft's Internet Explorer® Main Menu

In Internet Explorer®, move your mouse cursor to the tools menu and single left click on the menu. Move your mouse cursor down to where it says Internet options and single left click on that. Then the Internet options menu should show up like the picture shown on the next page:

Microsoft's Internet Explorer® 8 Options Menu

In Microsoft's Internet Explorer®, move your mouse cursor to the tab at the top of the pop up window where it says "General" in the options pop up window and single left click on it. There is a text box where it says "Home Page". Erase what is in that text box and type in the web page that you wish to be the default or home page, move your mouse cursor to the "ok" button and single left click on it. Your default home page has now been set to the web page that you have typed into the home page text box.

And that's it! That is how you set the default or home page for the browser of your choice. From now on, the first web page that comes up when will be the web page of your choice and not the one that got programmed in when you the web browser got installed on your computer.

Chapter Four:

Using And Fully Utilizing Electronic Mail (E-Mail)

Chapter Four: Using and Fully Utilizing Electronic Mail (E-Mail)

Electronic Mail or E-Mail changed how people communicate from the business world, to families that live far away to easily stay in touch. E-Mail allows you not only to send letters to people; also send pictures and more recently small video clips. Many people already know how to send an e-mail, but not fully utilizing the powers of e-mail. This chapter will attempt to do that. We will like in other chapters, build your skills from the ground up.

This chapter covers Windows Mail for Windows 7. Also there are many webmail services out there like Yahoo mail, Google's Gmail, and Microsoft's Hotmail. These services also give you e-mail which gives you the distinct advantage of not tying you to just the e-mail address that your Internet Service Provider has given you and with these services, you can check and write email from any computer or device with an internet connection.

Note – Microsoft has decided at the time of this writing to not bundle Windows Mail with Windows 7. If you want to still install Windows mail to use for your e-mail program, start up Internet Explorer and go to http://download.live.com/, single left click on the "Download" button to download the Essentials package that includes Windows Live Mail, Windows Live Movie Maker, and other programs as shown in the picture shown below.

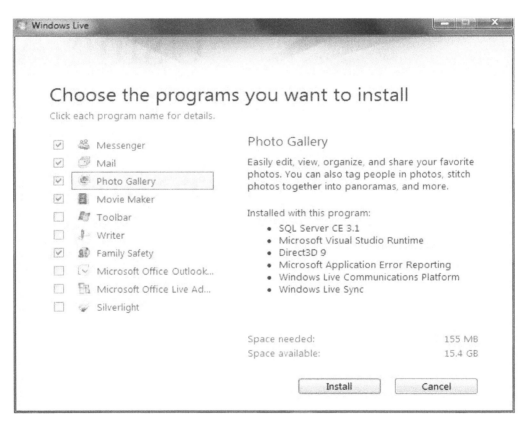

Even though these online services will not be covered in this chapter, you can follow along and the features in most cases, are the same as in Windows Mail®. Before we get into working with these Windows Mail, we have to Windows Mail to work with the E-Mail address your Internet Service Provider has given you to use. The 4 things we will need to get your account to work are listed below:

1. Your Internet Service POP Server address (POP stands for Post Office Protocol). It handles E-Mail coming in from people that has sent you E-Mail.

2. Your Internet Service SMTP Server address (SMTP stands for Simple Mail Transfer Protocol). This is used to send messages and forwards that you have written to people.

3. The username you gave the Internet service provider to setup your Internet account with them.

4. Also the password that you gave the Internet service provider to setup your Internet account with them.

If you don't remember or lost the documentation that they gave to you, you are going to have to call the customer service of the Internet Service Provider that you have to get this information, because you are going to need it to get Windows Mail® to send and receive E-Mails at all. When we have this information, we can move on to the next step: setting up the e-mail program itself.

<u>Setting Up Your E-Mail Account On Windows Mail</u>

To setup the e-mail account for your Internet Service Provider, start up Windows Mail® and go through the setup wizard to input the information from them. First single left click the start menu and single left click on the "All Programs" section of the start menu. Move your mouse cursor to the Windows Live folder and single left click on it. The Windows Live menu pops up and you can then single left click on Windows Mail.

Windows Mail® will start up and if it is the first time that you started up this program, a setup wizard starts up like in the pictures shown below. We will go step by step in setting up your e-mail account to work with Windows Mail®.

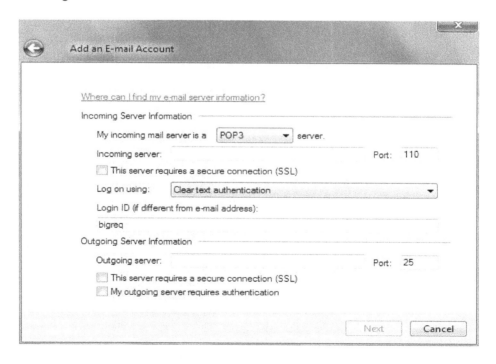

Add an E-mail Account

Please enter your e-mail account information below:

E-mail address:

example555@hotmail.com   Get a free e-mail account

Password:

☑ Remember password

How should your name appear in e-mail sent from this account?

Display Name:

For example: John Smith

☐ Manually configure server settings for e-mail account.

Next   Cancel

This screen is the first step in the Windows Mail® wizard where they ask you to type in e-mail address and your name In the Display Name Box. Type in the e-mail address your Internet Service Provider had given to you. It is usually username@yourinternetserviceprovidername.com .org or .net. Then type in your name in the Display Name box. Single left click on "Manually configure server settings for e-mail account" box and single left click on the next button at the bottom of the window.

Add an E-mail Account

Where can I find my e-mail server information?

Incoming Server Information

My incoming mail server is a   POP3 ▼ server.

Incoming server: Port: 110
☐ This server requires a secure connection (SSL)

Log on using: Clear text authentication ▼

Login ID (if different from e-mail address):

bigreq

Outgoing Server Information

Outgoing server: Port: 25
☐ This server requires a secure connection (SSL)
☐ My outgoing server requires authentication

Next   Cancel

58

The second screen is the second step in Windows Mail® where they ask you to type in the POP and SMTP information that we need from the Internet Service Provider so the program could connect to the right servers to deliver and to send E-Mail. Type in the POP information in the Incoming Server text box and the SMTP information in the Outgoing Server text box and single left click on the next button at the bottom of the window. Now we have everything setup, let's get started with fully utilizing the power that is E-Mail.

The Main Screens Of Your E-Mail Program

Windows Mail Main Screen

As you can see, This program is divided into three sections

- The left section of the main window lists the folders that Windows Mail sets up during configuration such as:

  1. Inbox – Holds Your Incoming E-Mails
  2. Sent/Sent Items – Stores copies of messages that you have sent to people
  3. Drafts – Stores drafts of messages that you were working on, but haven't sent yet
  4. Deleted/Deleted Items – Contains E-Mails that have been deleted

- The middle section of the main window shows the list of e-mails that are in your Inbox. The inbox holds messages that have been downloaded from your Internet Service Provider and e-mails that you have not checked previously or deleted.

- The right section of the main window is called the "Preview" window. It displays the contents of the message that is currently selected from the top section window.

59

Sending E-Mails

To create a email in Windows Mail, single left click on the "New" button. The button is located at the top toolbar in the program just below the file menu. A new mail message screen will pop up.

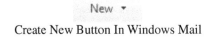

Create New Button In Windows Mail

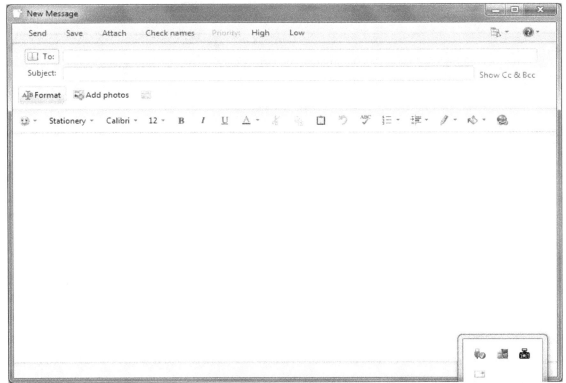

New Mail Message -Windows Mail

To create a message, have the person's e-mail handy. Make sure the spelling of the e-mail is correct because your message will not be sent at all if the spelling is incorrect. The steps below are how you would compose the e-mail in either program

1. First, move your cursor to the "To:" textbox, single left click on it. Type that e-mail address of the person that you want to send this message to in the textbox. Again, make sure that the e-mail address is correctly spelled, or the message will not be sent at all.

2. Secondly, move your cursor to the "Subject:" textbox and single left click on it. Type a brief summary of what this e-mail is about in the textbox.

3. Thirdly, move your cursor to the blank box on the bottom of the window and single left click on it. Type the actual message in this box.

4. When you are done typing your actual message to this recipient of this message, move your mouse to the send button and single left click on it. Your E-Mail message will then be sent to that e-mail address you inputted. That is how you put together and send an e-mail message.

Sending Attachments In E-Mails

Attachments are files on your computer that you want to send to people. Pictures, Documents and other files are considered attachments. Here's how to e-mail documents, spreadsheets, photos or any other type of file.

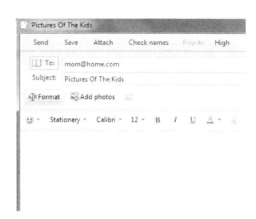

1. Open your e-mail program, launch a new message window and compose your message.

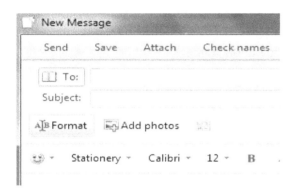

2. Single left click the **"Attach"** button on the top toolbar menu or the "Add Photos" link button.

3. Browse your hard drive or <u>removable disks</u> to locate the **file** you want to attach. Single left click it to highlight the name, and then click the **Open** button.

61

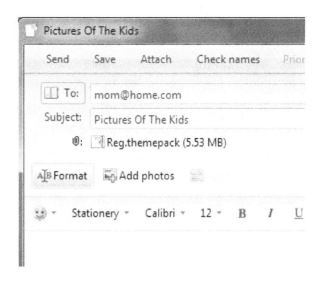

4. An icon or message should now appear indicating that the file has been attached.

5. Finally, single left click the **Send** button and off it goes!

That's how you send attachments in E-Mail messages!

Opening E-Mail Messages

When you are at the main screen of Windows Mail, move your cursor to a specific message on the top part of the program and single left click on the actual message. The message will come up in the right window so that you can read the actual message.

Replying To E-Mails

While in that message that is opened in either e-mail program, you will notice a button that says Reply . Single left click on that button and a window will allow you to type in that same e-mail message what you want to say in response to a particular e-mail. After you have typed in what you wanted to say in response, then single left click the "Send" button. The e-mail will be sent back to the original person who sent the message.

Forwarding E-Mail

While in that message, if you find that this message would interest someone else that you know, you can send it to them hence the term "Forwarding". you do that by single left clicking a button that says Forward . A window pops up where you can add the e-mail address of the person who you want to send this message to. Insert the e-mail address of the person you want to in the "To" text box and single left click on the "Send" button. This message is now sent to the person.

Deleting E-Mail

On the main screen of the e-mail program, move your cursor to the message you would want to delete and single left click on it. Then move your cursor up to the Delete button in Windows Mail and single left click on it. The message will now be deleted.

Keeping People & E-Mail Addresses In Your Contact/Address Book

The main reason behind using an address book is to store and maintain information about individuals. After creating entries in an address book, you can use address book to look up information about your personal contacts, such as email addresses and phone numbers. From the main window in the main window of the Windows Mail, single left click on the "Contacts" button on the bottom left part of the main window in Windows Mail. The contacts window will come up as shown in the picture below.

To add a contact to the list, move your mouse cursor to the upper left part of this window and single left click on the "New" button. A drop menu will come up and single left click on the "Contact" menu choice as shown in the picture on the next page:

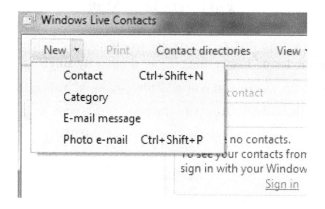

A new contact window will come up as shown in the picture below:

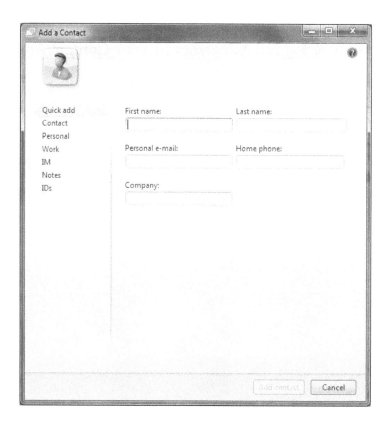

Fill out the information for this person and single left click on the "Add Contact" button. That particular individual contact information is now in the address book as shown in the next picture.

Now that you have a contact in your address book, If you want to send a email to them without typing in their e-mail address all of the time, in the new e-mail window, single left click on the "To" button, and your address book will come up. Find the person in the address book that you want to send the e-mail to and double left click on that name, single left click the "OK" button and then the name will then be placed in the "To" textbox.

Adding Signatures To Your E-Mails

Signatures are comments or information that you could have automatically appear at the bottom of every e-mail so that you don't have to repeatedly type it in. On the menus option, single left click The Options menu choice as shown in the picture below:

The options menu then comes up. Locate and single left click on the Signatures tab. The signatures menu will come up like the picture shown:

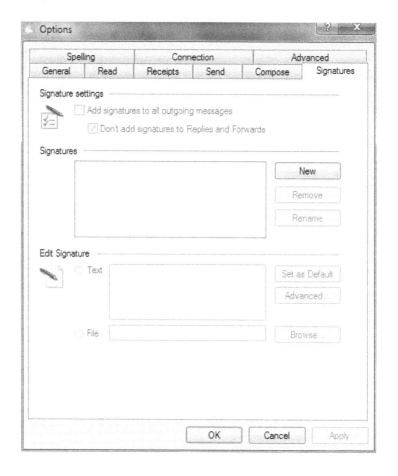

1. To create a signature, single left click the New button and then enter text in the Edit Signature box.

2 . Select the Add signatures to all outgoing messages check box.

3. Single left click on the OK button. Now your signature should show at the bottom of every new e-mail you create now.

I hope that this chapter has clarified how to use the most useful features in E-Mail and you can now utilize e-mail for your personal, work or business use.

Chapter Five:

The Critical Task Of Backing Up Your Computer

Chapter Five: The Critical Task of Backing/Restoring Your Computer

Let me begin by saying that doing backups correctly is crucial to being confident that if anything happens to your computer such as a hard drive failure, virus or malware attack, you don't lose all of your files. Like I had stated about your (C:) drive being like a file cabinet, we can consider a good backup to be like a fireproof safe.

The best way of doing your backups is to use a large flash drive (16GB or Larger) or an external hard drive you attach to your computer through an usb port. So now you're wondering "How do I start backing up my computer?" Well, there's many products at retail stores that you can buy that does backups, and I tried many of them, but none of them seemed simple to use, not until I discovered a utility called Fab's Autobackup.

Fab's Autobackup is on the utilities CD. Insert the CD into your CD-ROM Drive by pressing on the eject button on the CD/DVD Rom on the computer. The CD/DVD ROM Drive will eject.

Place the CD/DVD ROM in the drive, label side up and press the eject button again on the CD/DVD ROM to close the drive. The computer will read the CD and then the autoplay menu pops up when the computer recognizes that a CD has been inserted into the computer as shown in the pictures below:

Auto play Feature In Windows 7®

Select the "Open Folder To View Files" Menu and a window will pop open to show everything that is on that CD-ROM. Double Left click Autobackup, and the program will open up a window that looks like the following picture shown:

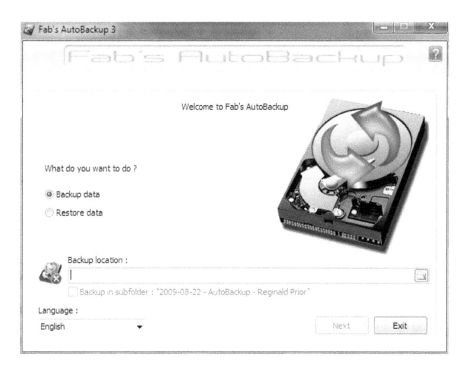

Like I had said previously in Chapter One, make sure when you work on your computer is to make sure that you save your files in one of these folders

- Documents
- Music
- Pictures

The reason why is when you use Autobackup or any other backup program, it backup things from those folders. If things are in other places on the (C:) drive, it is a pretty slim chance your files will be successfully backed up. To start backing up the computer using Autobackup, attach your external hard drive or flash drive to the computer to one of the usb ports.

Autobackup asks you if you want to backup or restore data. In this case, we are backing up, so move your mouse cursor to the "Backup Data" option, single left click on it, then single left click on the icon that looks like a folder under the "Backup Location" textbox. A window will pop up looking like the picture below asking you where to save the backups.

In this window, you would single left click the arrow next to "Computer" and find the removable flash drive that you inserted into your computer in this list. Single left click on the flash drive and Single left click on the "OK" button. This will take you back to the main fabs autobackup screen. Check the "Save in Subfolder" box and single left click on the "Next" button. The next steps include windows on which folders you want to have backed up.

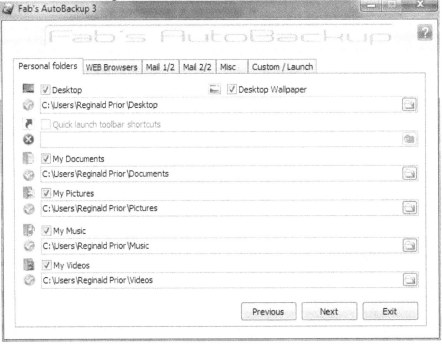

This is the first window in Autobackup. This window deals with what to backup in your personal folders, including desktop settings and documents. Single left click on the next button.

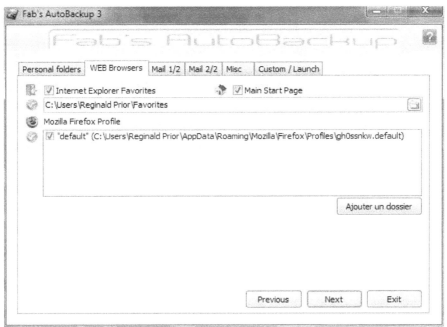

This is the second window in Autobackup. This window is concerned with backing up your web browser settings including favorites and your default start page. Single left click on the next button.

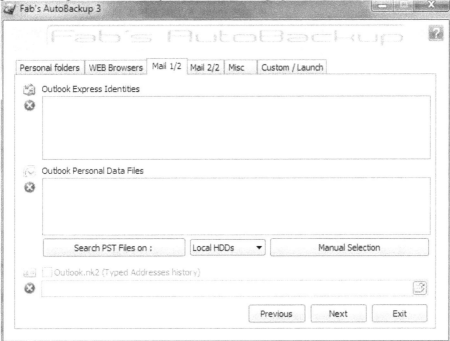

This is the third window in Autobackup. This window is concerned about backing up your Windows Mail settings and E-Mails. Single left click on the next button.

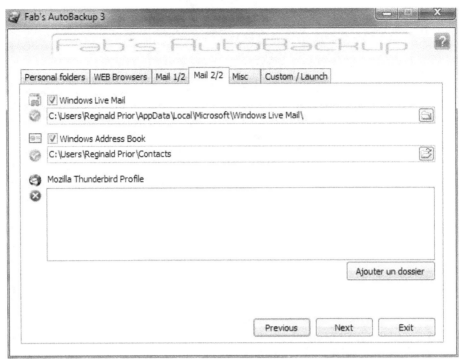

This is the fourth window in Autobackup. This window is the second part of backing up your Windows Mail. This section backups your address book. Single left click on the next button.

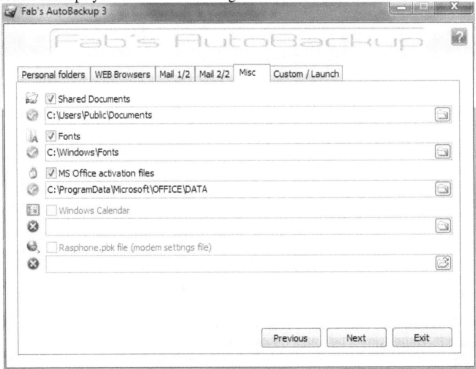

This is the fifth window in Autobackup. This window backups your fonts and any shared documents on the computer. Single left click on the next button.

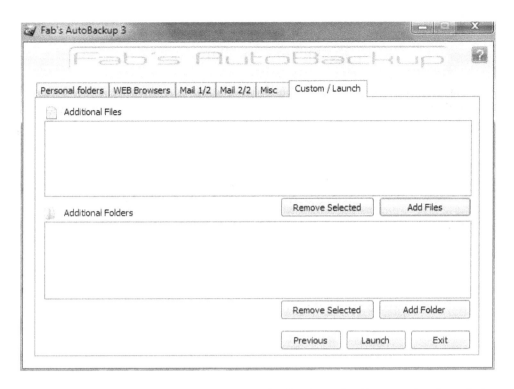

This is the final window in the Autobackup wizard. Single left click on the launch button to start backing up your data to your flash drive.

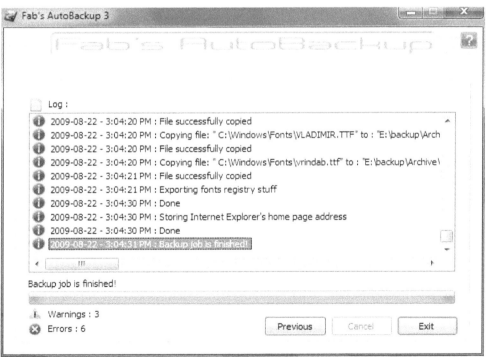

The data is now being backed up to the external hard drive or flash drive. When this process is successful, you have now backed up your computer. Single left click the "Exit" button and the program will close. Not that hard now was it? ☺

Restoring Your Backups

To restore your backups or transfer them to another computer, plug in the USB flash drive or the external hard drive that you had backed up to in the USB Drive of the computer. Place the utilities CD-ROM back into the computer and open back up the Fab's Autobackup program. When the main window comes back up, single left click on the "Restore Data" option in the window. The Screen will now look like the picture shown below:

Single left click on the icon that looks like a folder under the "Backup Location" textbox. A window that asks you what drive to select will come up like the picture shown below:

Where your USB external hard drive or flash drive comes up as Removable Drive (Drive Letter:) single left click on the arrow symbol to the left of the drive. The contents of the drive will show below when you click on the plus symbol. Autobackup does a beautiful thing when it creates backups. It shows the user that it backed up, and dates the backup so you know exactly when the backup was done.

Single left click on the latest backup folder on the drive and single left click the "OK" button. On the main menu, Single left click on the last tab "Personnalise" on the main screen as shown in the picture below:

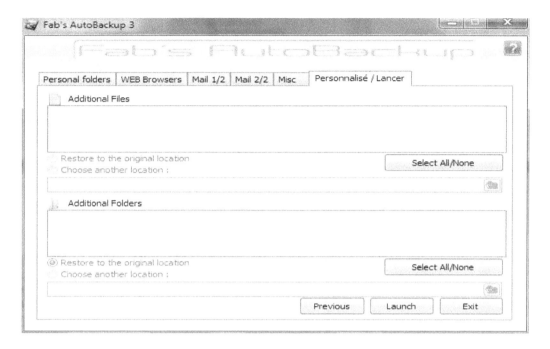

Then single left click on the "Restore" Button. All of your documents, settings, etc will be transferred back on the computer. After that has been done, click the "Exit" button and the program will close.

Now that you know how simple it can be to backup and restore your computer, it is very important that you do this exercise at least twice a month, so that you do not lose everything that had been on your computer. There has been countless times where I had to tell people that it was nothing I could do to recover pictures or documents from years past they had stored on the computer when the hard drive totally failed on their computer and would not power up at all.

We are about to move onto the last chapter in this book which will answer a lot of questions I get all of the time from people such as yourself such as "How do I protect my computer from viruses or malware" or "How do I keep my computer running its best" Well, I am about to explain everything in the next chapter "Computer Maintenance and Upkeep"

Chapter Six:

Computer Maintenance And Upkeep

Chapter Six: Computer Maintenance and Upkeep

This is going to be a chapter on what you can do to keep your computer running at optimal performance and put yourself at minimum risk of getting a virus or malware on your computer. When I meet with people for the first time and take a look at their computers, often I see no protection programs installed at all. Listed below are the programs that you HAVE to have installed, ESPECIALLY if this computer is connected to the internet at all.

First, you have to have an antivirus program installed on your computer and update often. This may seem simple, but I have seen computers a lot of times without anything on them or the antivirus program on them is as old as the computer. You have to get a new version of the antivirus program EVERY YEAR! Thousands of viruses are written everyday and released on the internet. If you are not installing a new version of these antivirus programs every year, you are putting yourself at risk of having your computer attacked by a virus.

They are many antivirus programs out there on the market. Examples of anti-virus programs are:

- Norton Antivirus (Part of the Norton 360 Suite) at http://www.symantec.com

- McAfee Antivirus (Part of their Internet Security Suite) at http://www.mcafee.com

But the one I recommend is the AVG antivirus program at http://free.grisoft.com and on the utilities CD. Usually I do not suggest a program that is free, but I used Norton and McAfee over the years and I have found that not only AVG catches more viruses, but AVG does not affect your computers performance. These all-in-one suites don't do a complete job protecting your computer and actually slows down your computer. I find that one program that tries to do everything really is not good at anything. Shown on the next page is what the AVG antivirus program looks like:

AVG Antivirus Version 8

To update AVG, First double left click on the AVG shortcut on your desktop. When the main menu comes up, single left click on the link on the left side of the window that says "Update Now" and the program will check for updates and if there is an update, show a pop-up screen like the one shown in the picture below:

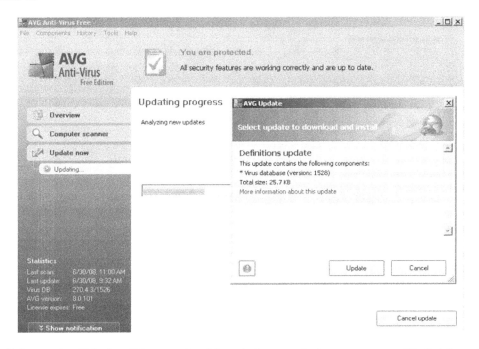

Single left click on the "Update" button in this window and the program will finish updating itself. Simple as that!

You can tryout the other suites mentioned above; everything is a matter of preference. The point that I am trying to make is that you have to install an antivirus program on your computer and update with the newest version EVERY YEAR. Computers are just like a car, you have to keep up with maintenance to keep it running its best!

The second program that I would suggest installing along with the antivirus program and update regularly is an anti-malware scanner of some type. There are programs out there that eliminate spyware such as:

- Ad-Aware at http://www.lavasoft.com/
- Spybot Search And Destroy at http://www.safer-networking.org/en/index.html

I have been using these two programs together for years, but have found a program that does the same thing in one program than with these two called Malware bytes located at http://www.malwarebytes.org/ and on the utilities CD. Shown on the next page is a picture of the main screen of malware bytes:

79

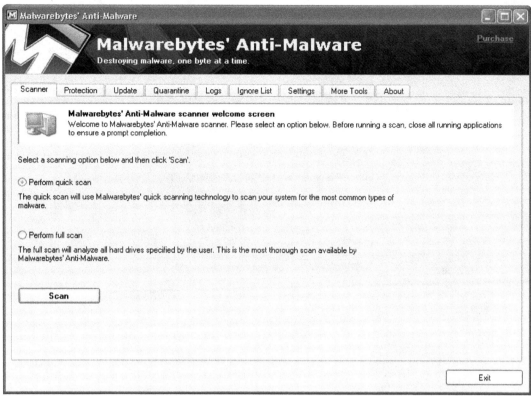

Malware Bytes Anti-Malware Main Screen.

To scan your computer for malware that maybe on your computer, single left click on either "Perform Quick Scan" or "Perform Full Scan" options with your mouse cursor and single left click on the "Scan" button. The program scans your computer for potential problems. To update the malware bytes program, move your mouse cursor to the third tab "Update" on the top and single left click on it. Your screen should look like the picture shown below:

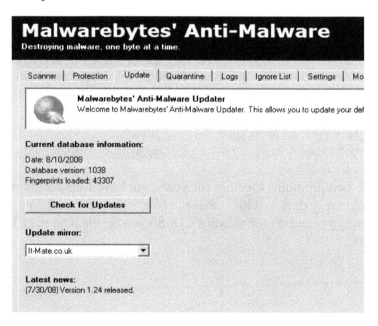

Single left click on the "Check for Updates" button and the program will check for updates and install them if there are any. But these are the two programs you need to have installed on your computer, update and scan your computer in order to effectively keep your computer running at its best. I would talk about installing a firewall, but Microsoft already has a firewall installed. Also your internet router also has a firewall installed on it. There is no need to add another firewall onto your computer and risk slowing your internet and computer down.

I almost forgot to make this point – The most crucial thing you can do to not to have problems with your computer is NOT TO USE FREE MUSIC DOWNLOADING PROGRAMS SUCH AS LIMEWIRE, KAZAA OR FROSTWIRE!!!! Viruses and Malware live on these sites and are the fastest ways that you can get your computer infected. You can buy your music very cheaply through http://www.amazon.com or at iTunes at http://www.Apple.com/itunes/. Lately on the news (MSNBC) , hackers have successfully exploited the program to scan computers hard drives and to gain access to peoples tax return information among other things. The story starts on the next page:

P2P networks threaten home PC security

Media-sharing software loaded by kids can expose trove of financial data

Tami Olson's oldest daughter exposed the family's financial records online when she installed a popular music-sharing software package.

By Jeremy Brilliant and Holly Stephen
NBC News

INDIANAPOLIS - Users of peer-to-peer platforms, also known as P2P networks, may be under attack from entertainment lawyers policing copyright violations, but they can also be an easy target for identity thieves. And they may never know about it if it's their kids who load the software.

Take the Olsons, a typical Indiana family: Christopher and Tami have three daughters, as well as a family dog.

The dog's name can't yet be found online, but everyone else's can, thanks to security holes in popular P2P music downloading software. So can their birthdates and the family's income and banking information.

 "Unbelievable ... how did it get out there?" asked Tami Olson, who pays bills and does her taxes online.

The Olsons' private data were found through LimeWire, a software program used to download music and videos. Within a matter of minutes, two of the Olsons' tax returns were available.

"Well, this is our entire tax history. It's going to have, I imagine, the Social Security number of my husband, myself and our three children right there," Tami Olson said.

She was right. In addition to the family's income, the data included banking and routing numbers.

With the expansion of broadband service making it easier to share large media files, more than 60 million Americans have downloaded and used P2P services like LimeWire and Kazaa, according to the Federal Trade Commission and the Electronic Frontier Foundation, a digital-rights group.

The Olsons' oldest daughter unknowingly exposed the family's personal and financial records after downloading LimeWire. "She didn't really think there was anything wrong with that," her mother said. "I told them to get it off immediately because I have a lot of personal info out there."

Total exposure
Many users don't realize that when they use file-sharing software, they are putting their hard drives on the network, to be shared with anyone else using the network.

Users can specify what files are private, but many don't, said Eugene Spafford, a computer science professor at Purdue University and executive director of the Center for Education and Research in Information Assurance and Security.

"One problem with peer-to-peer is getting the settings wrong and sharing your entire disk or your entire personal file system, rather than simply the files you think you're sharing," Spafford said.

"We've created a culture and an expectation that you just install the software and you never bother to read that license that comes up or the warnings that come up," he said.

Spafford said the Olsons' story was not unique.

"Parents don't understand the technology well enough to talk to their kids," he said. Security experts say it's easy to exploit such vulnerabilities because data can be found through simple search strings, like "[bank name] July statement" or "[bank name] routing information."

'Giving criminals the keys to your computer'
Just this month, a Seattle man was charged with identity theft in a case that illustrates just how glaring such vulnerabilities are.

The man, Gregory Kopiloff, used LimeWire, the same software used by the Olsons, to dig into hundreds of hard drives, prosecutors said. He was accused of harvesting tax returns and student aid forms from at least 83 people and buying $73,000 in merchandise through fake credit card accounts he set up using the data.

Investigators said most of the victims had teenage children and did not know the software was even on their computers.

"If you are running file-sharing software, you are giving criminals the keys to your computer," Assistant U.S. Attorney Kathryn Warma said. "Criminals are getting access to incredibly valuable information."

Not fully understanding the P2P risks can also open the door for others to use your hard drive to hide evidence of their own crimes.

"If you've got a Machine, do you know what's in every directory on your Machine?" Spafford asked. "Probably not.

"These criminals will take those Machines and store the contraband material on them, because they know if a warrant is served on their home and they're found with that on their disk, they can be prosecuted."

Getting hit with the news that you're a victim of identity theft is becoming more common. The Federal Trade Commission says as many as 9 million Americans' identities are stolen every year. So how do you protect your computer files from P2P identity theft? Know what's installed on your computer, and take the time to look at the security settings. Tami Olson said she had learned the lesson.

"Obviously, I'm going to be more careful about what I store in my computer," she said. "If my kids are going to download in the future, I want to be there. I want to read what they're downloading."

Chapter Seven:

Taking Back Control Of Your Computer

Chapter Seven: Taking Back Control of Your Computer

Over the years, many people, especially parents that have computer savvy children asked me that if anything could be installed on their computer to monitor and have more control over what their children can or cannot do on the family computer, and on the Internet at home. And up to that point, there was no simplistic or easy way to do so.

There are some products out on the market such as net nanny that monitored what users see on the Internet, but they sort of worked to varying degrees. But there was no way of controlling what users do to the computer itself outside the Windows user account settings, so the owners of computers were still having issues with other people downloading illegal music sharing programs, viruses, malware and other programs onto their computer.

Microsoft must have listened to these frustrations from users of Windows, especially parents of children who really wanted to know what their children were doing on their home computers. So they have implemented the new Family Live Safety Suite which allows parents to:

• Set up web filtering to allow only the content you want your kids to see. Use contact management to choose who they talk to online when they use Windows Live Messenger, Windows Live Hotmail, and Windows Live Spaces. You can customize settings for each family member.

• Manage your kids' safety settings from any computer, and get Web-based reports that show what your kids are doing online. You can grant or deny requests to view specific Web sites from almost any computer online.

• Steer your kids toward appropriate websites. Also set time limits that you desire your children to be able to use the computer

In this chapter, we will go over in detail how to utilize these powerful features to take back control of your computer! To get started using these great features, you need to first go to the Microsoft's Windows 7 Essentials Website, which is located at http://download.live.com/familysafety or insert the Reg's Practical Guide Utilities CD to download and install the Microsoft Live Essentials programs which includes the Family Safety filter you need to have installed on your computer to be able to move forward in this chapter.

To take back control of your computer, you need to understand that they are three phases to taking back control of your computer. I will go step by step into the individual phases:

The First Phase:

The first phase of taking back control of your computer consists of setting time limits on when certain users are allowed to use the computer at all. Microsoft has added enhanced user controls to Windows 7 for you to be able to set specified hours for other users outside of yourself to use the computer.

To enable the settings to limit computer time, First move your mouse cursor to the Start menu and single left click on it. Move your mouse cursor to the control panel option and single left click on it. The control panel should come up like the picture shown below:

Move your mouse cursor to the "User Accounts and Family Safety" link and single left click on it. The next screen should look like the picture shown below:

Move your mouse cursor and Single left click on the "User Accounts" link. The settings for the current user should come up in the next screen. More than likely, it is another user account that you have setup that you would want to monitor, so you would have to tell Windows to set controls on another account.

So what you will do is move your mouse cursor over to the "Manage Another Account" link in that window and single left click on it. The window should look like the following picture shown below:

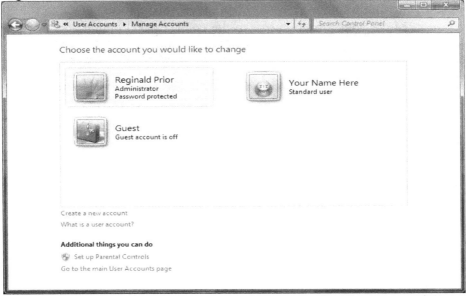

Note – If you haven't created a separate user account for a user other than yourself, it would be a good idea to go back to chapter two and read the section "Adding/Changing Users In Windows" to add a separate account for that user.

The user that I want to set the restrictions for in this case is the account that I had created on this computer named "Your Name Here". So move my mouse to that account icon and single left click on that account. The detailed user account information window should come up like the window shown below:

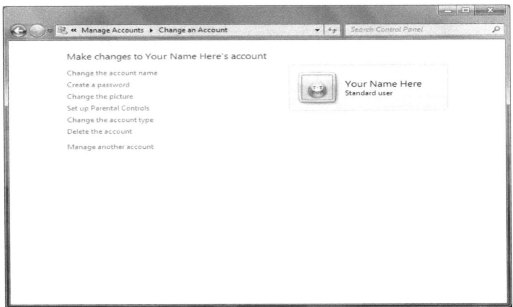

Move your mouse cursor to the "Set up Parental Controls" link and single left click on it. The parental controls main menu will come up like the picture shown below:

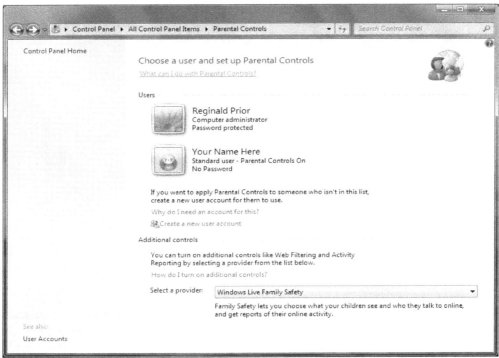

Move your mouse cursor to the account that you want to enforce the time settings on and single left click on it. The parental settings main menu window for this particular account should come up looking like the window shown below:

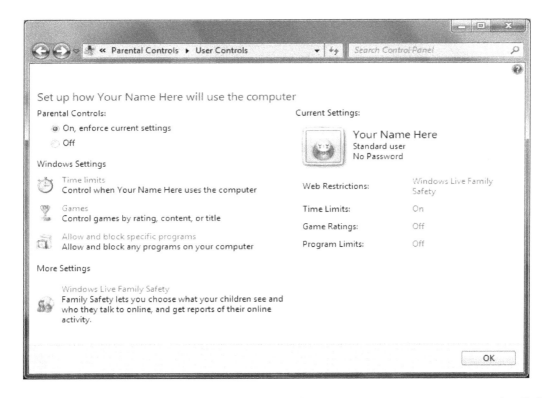

In this window, you should see a link called "Time Limits". Move your mouse cursor to that link and single left click on it. In this window, you would use your mouse and single left click to block out the times that this user is not to be signed onto the computer.

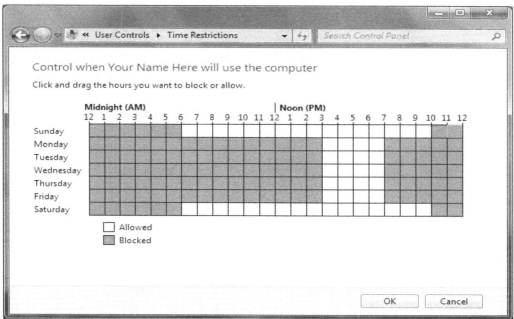

In the last window, I have limited the computer usage time for the user "Your Name Here" to be able to use the computer Monday thru Friday from 3PM to 7PM and on the weekends from 6AM to 10PM. You can set the time limits to your satisfaction and single left click on the "OK" button to save the desired usage time for that particular user. This takes care of phase one of taking back control of your computer. We now move on to the Second Phase – Restricting use of computer software.

The Second Phase:

You might be asking yourself "Why would I suggest limiting the programs on the computer that other users can use?" The answer is pretty simple. Many people who are trying to get around restrictions on a computer usually would download and install or use other programs on the computer to try to get around the restrictions. And if you limit the programs that they can use to get around the restrictions, the better and safer your computer would be.

On the parental settings main menu window, move your mouse cursor over to and single left click on the "Allow and Block Specific Programs" link. A window will come up and ask you if this user is allowed to use all of the programs on the computer (Not Recommended) or Use the programs that I allow.

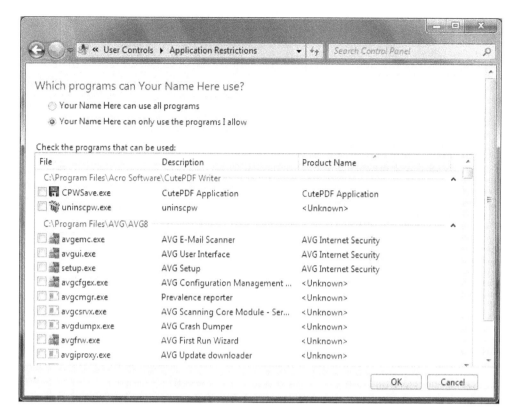

Single left click on the choice where it says that the user can only use the programs I allow. The computer will then scan for programs that are currently installed on this computer, and show them in this list. Most users usually only use three programs on the computer. Examples of those programs can be:

1. E-Mail
2. Internet Browsing
3. Word Processing (Typing Documents In Microsoft Word)

Everything else on the computer is not necessary for other users to access to operate the computer. The more programs other users have access to, the more likely that they can find loopholes in these programs to do other things to the computer. So what you would do in this window is scroll through this list and move your mouse cursor to the checkboxes on the left of the programs that allows users to do the tasks listed above and single left click on the checkbox to allow them to use that program. Everything else can be left unchecked.

When you are done tweaking these settings, move your mouse cursor to the "OK" button and single left click on it. You will return to the parental settings main menu window.

The Third And Final Phase:

The final and most important phase of taking back control of your computer is limiting the access to websites. The internet is a great tool for doing many things such as research among other things. But it is also a place where bad things can happen also. Like I explained in chapter six, Identity theft is the fastest growing crime and it is not getting better any time soon.

Programs like Frostwire, Limewire shares files between computers on the Internet can put you at risk for identity theft, viruses and other things. The best way to protect yourself this is to limit users from going to those websites to download and install the programs in the first place. And parents of children does not want their children being exposed to things that are freely on the Internet such as dating websites, pornographic material among other things.

Like I had stated at the beginning of this chapter, Microsoft has implemented in Windows 7 the new Family Live Safety Suite. This allows you not only to limit the access to certain websites, you can track other activity that the user is doing on the computer itself such as which programs are being used on the computer and if they are downloading files and other things.

You implement changes in the Live Family Suite by the parental settings main menu of the account you want to put restrictions on, move your mouse cursor over to the Windows Live Family Safety Link and single left click on it. Since this is the first time that you are setting up restrictions on this account, A log in window will come up like the picture shown on the next page asking you to sign up for the Windows Live Website.

You would need to sign up for this free service. This website allows you to change settings from any computer on the Internet and also view activity reports at any time. Also your other users can request access to certain websites which you can approve or deny from this service.

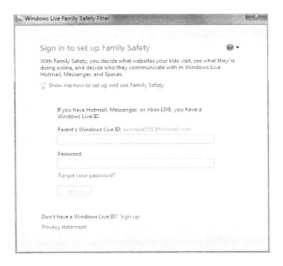

Move your mouse cursor over to the blue "Sign Up" link to be redirected to the Windows live website to sign up for this free service. The webpage would look like the picture shown on the next page:

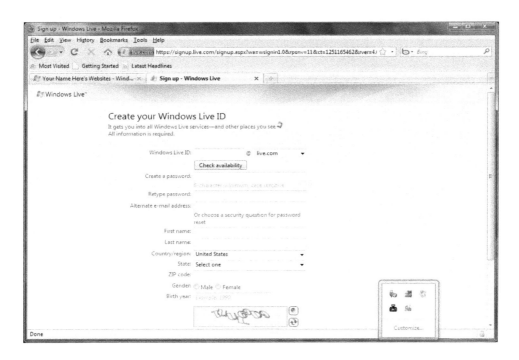

After you have signed up for the Windows Live Service, You can go back to the family safety sign in window as shown in the picture below, and enter in the textboxes the e-mail address and the password that you entered for signing up for the service and move your mouse cursor and single left clicking on the "Sign In" button.

The main screen that allows you to restrict websites that users can view looks like the picture on the next page:

Note – After you have setup everything on the computer for the first time, you can go on any computer that is connected to the Internet and point the web browser to http://fss.live.com/ and use your username and password to sign into the website and make changes and view all activity on demand.

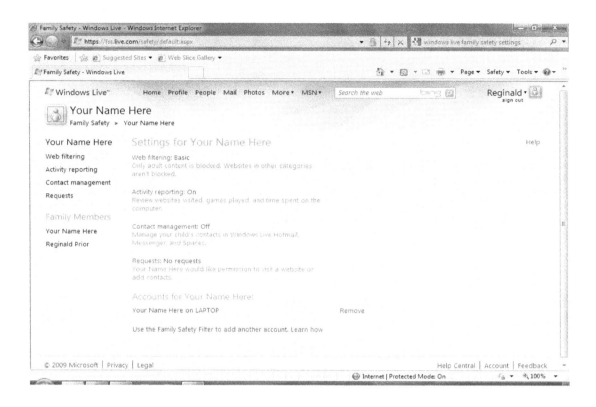

As you can see on the main page for Windows Live Family Safety website, you have four sections on where you can customize how and what you want to have monitored for each user that is on the family computer. Here's a short overview about which each section does to protect your computer.

Web Filtering – Web filtering allows you to control what content is delivered over the <u>Web</u>. This puts you totally in charge about which websites other users are allowed to see. To enable a web filter for a specific user, first move your mouse cursor to the user under the "Family Members" section of the webpage and single left click on it. Secondly, move your mouse cursor to the "Web Filtering" link and single left click on it. The webpage should look like the picture shown on the next page:

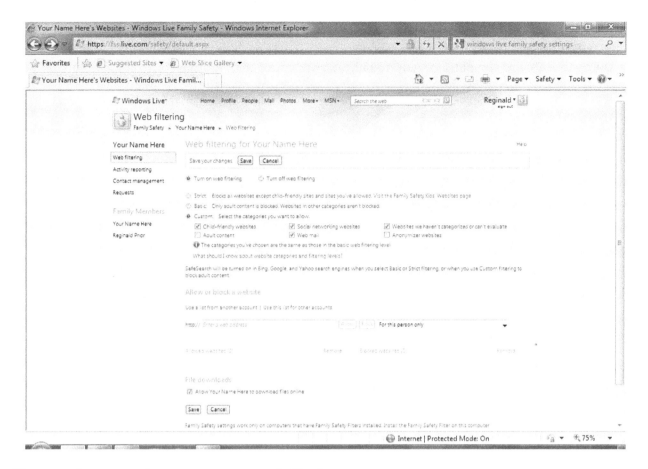

There are three ways that you can set up web filtering:

Strict (Not Recommended) – This setting really blocks just about every webpage except ones that Microsoft has deemed Kid Friendly. This list is located at http://fss.live.com/kids/

Basic – This setting blocks all adult content, but allows many other types of websites such as social networking (myspace.com, facebook.com, twitter.com)

Custom – This setting allows you to customize filtering by which types of websites other users are allowed to see or not to see.

My suggestion is to set the filtering to the Basic level and under the "Allow or Block a Website" manually type in a webpage that you don't want your other users to visit. You can tweak around with the settings in this section until you get the desired filters for the other users on this computer. When you are done with setting up web filtering, move your mouse cursor to the "Save" button and single left click on it. Your web filtering settings will be saved and implemented on the computer the next time that user signs into the computer.

Activity Reporting – View reports on computer activities for each user. You would know if other users are trying to hack the computer or get around the restrictions that you have set on the computer at a moments notice. The Activity Reporting screen looks like the picture shown below:

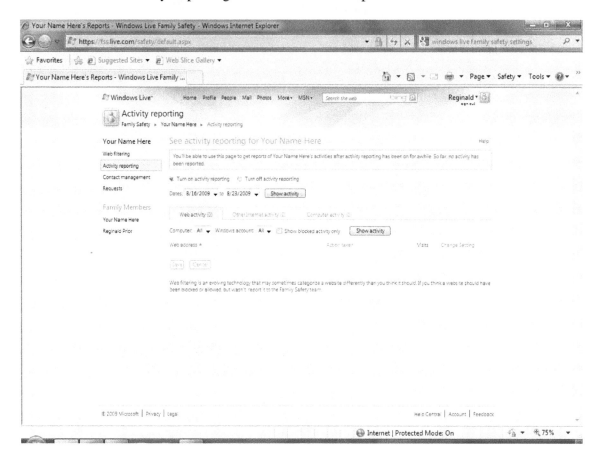

Contact Management – Contact Management helps you know who your kids are talking to in e-mail or blogs on Windows Live Spaces, or in IM on Windows Live Messenger. Contact management allows you to approve or reject each new contact. The contact management screen looks like the picture shown on the next page:

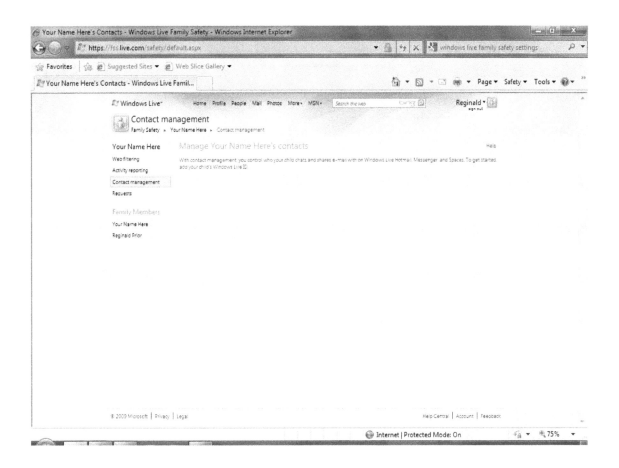

Requests – Your users can request access to blocked websites by clicking on a link to send you an e-mail so that you can research the requested website before allowing or denying access to it. The picture shown below shows what a blocked website would look like on the users screen and how they would submit a request to you to unblock the website.

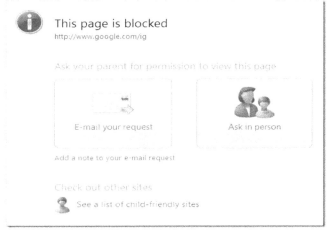

When the user requests access to a particular webpage, it will look like the following picture under the Windows Live Family Safety requests page:

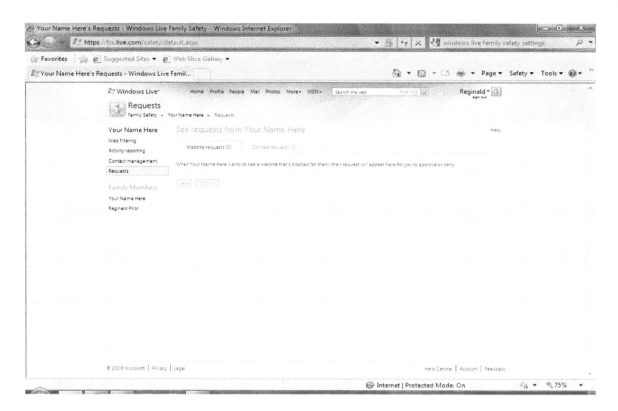

In this section, you will see all of the webpage requests from all of the users on your computer, you have the option now to allow access to that webpage or deny access to that website. This allows you as the administrator to investigate this webpage to make sure that it is a webpage that is acceptable to you and accept or deny the request as you see fit.

I hope that you have gained a lot of knowledge in learning more about your computer by reading this book. Just like in the preface, you are the most important critic and value all of your feedback about this book so that I can improve future texts. Thank you for reading and look forward to hearing from you!!

Works Cited

Jeremy Brilliant and Holly Stephen.
"P2P networks threaten home PC security."

MSNBC Online. 18 October 2007.
http://www.msnbc.msn.com/id/21364575/
3/17/2009

Notes

www.ingramcontent.com/pod-product-compliance
Lightning Source LLC
Chambersburg PA
CBHW082111070326
40689CB00052B/4503